ISBN: 9798832391830

Printed in the United States of America

First Edition

Cover Image by Cristina Prestin-Beard – Alcatraz Island (2018)

Finding Mercy in the Madness

Cristina Prestin-Beard

M.S., CFLE

To my daughters, Carleigh and Camryn:
Don't let statistics ever stand in your way...

Love Always,
Mom

Note to Readers:

This book has been designed to be interactive. You are encouraged to reflect upon your journey as you travel through mine. The margins and line spacing are intentionally wide. I wanted you to have room to write your thoughts, feelings, and share your own experiences.

I did not want my life story to be read as "half way through" or "twenty pages left" – so there are no page numbers. It is divided into five sections (Just Getting Started, Life in the Fast Lane, Keep on Truckin', The Long Haul, and The Road Less Traveled) to help guide you.

It took a lifetime to create this memoir and a huge amount of courage to release it publicly. I appreciate each and every one of you for taking your time to read it.

Best,
Cristina

Preface

Part One: Just Getting Started

Part Two: Life in the Fast Lane

Preface

The number of times I have sat down to start writing this memoir over the years have been countless. Something always has a way of taking over my time. I am sure many of you are familiar with that feeling. The constant running on life's treadmill that somedays feels like your legs have traveled miles. The overextending yourself – as a mother, a wife, a friend, a daughter and an employee. Each day – almost the same day – not bad, not spectacular – on repeat. Right?

Then the feelings of doubt would take over. This is a waste of time. No one cares about my journey. All lies. Do not fall victim to the critic in your mind. You are often your own worst enemy. I know this all too well.

People do care. They want to feel normal. When others realize you are just as messed up as they are, it brings them comfort. They find relief – a safe haven in knowing they are not alone with their mistakes, thoughts, and feelings. We are all human. Humans screw up.

Perhaps that is why I am finally sitting down to share my story. Hoping to keep walking – sprinting – probably tripping a few times due to lack of coordination – towards that light at the end of the tunnel . . . and trying to take you with me. Strap on your miner's helmet. We are digging our way out of here.

Before We Travel

Let's briefly address the title of this memoir. *Finding Mercy in the Madness* was picked specifically for the words "mercy" and "madness". Let's make things clear: when I speak of *mercy*, I mean forgiveness and compassion – for others – and especially for the self. This is hard. Like stupid hard. Your best friend dates a total douche bag and gets her heart broken – duh, saw that one coming. You are there to toss back a couple shots and remind her she was too good for him. Hug her through the ugly cry and fix the mascara mess. However, if you make the same epic screw up in your love life, you doom yourself to eternal loneliness and must be the biggest loser on the planet. It is easy to be kind to those we love in their time of need – but so hard to be that same compassionate person towards ourselves.

As for *madness*, I do not mean the full-on definition of insanity. More along the lines of chaotic and bizarre behavior. Perhaps this is by choice – self-inflicted has usually been my method. Although, this can be due to the behaviors of others, extenuating circumstances. Or, heck, when it feels like society as a whole has lost its marbles. I think you can relate to where I am coming from here.

Be sure to keep *mercy* and *madness* in mind throughout our time together. Not only as you are reading my own ups and downs, but when you are thinking of yours. Please allow me to put on my social scientist cap for a moment. College degrees cost a lot of money and I should attempt to make my parents proud.

Time and Space

I tell my students that we are the creatures of two things: time and space. Time, meaning the historical component of our lives. Our generation, the decades we live through – however you wish to state it. For example, we are all chartering the tail-end (fingers crossed) of a global pandemic. This impacts us – whether we were children or adults during this time. My grandfather (rest in peace, Sam) grew up during the Great Depression. Until the day he died, the man would lick a plate clean. If you had leftovers, he would eat those, too. Frankly, it was a disgusting thing to watch – but it makes sense. If you never know when you will get your next meal as a child, it affects you. Things he endured in his childhood carried with him throughout his entire life.

That happens. We carry things over. Generation to generation. Maybe it is Grandma's gravy boat that no one ever uses, maybe it's familial wealth, or that God awful wedding dress. Unfortunately, many times it is trauma, abuse or poverty.

So, what about space? No, not outer space. Don't get me started on aliens. Literally the location where you live on Earth. We all learned in kindergarten how life in another country varies from ours. No shit. Geographically, you do not have to think that large. My great state of Illinois can be viewed as the big gorgeous city of Chicago skylights. Or the demolished areas of Cabrini Green government housing being replaced with mixed income communities. My neck of the woods is a small town in rural Central Illinois – that literally has no stop lights. My life changed for the better when we finally got a Dollar General. I wish I had more exciting events to report, but that really was it for a few years of my life.

Not just the country, state or city. The household as well. Two kids growing up with the exact same street address can have very different upbringings and experiences.

The Big Tickets

It is pretty easy to look back on your life and think of, what I refer to as, the big-ticket items. This is your collection of large events that took place in your life. Graduations, break ups, babies, deaths. Car crashes, Taylor Swift announces another tour, finally getting your braces off.

Me? I never had braces. I still have a gap between my two front teeth. I have grown to love it. Lauren Hutten has gapped teeth and she is fabulous. My mother didn't want my teeth to 'look like everyone else's' so I did not have braces growing up. Great to squirt water like a fountain as a kid. Also, a great way to get picked on. Thank goodness I was a kid before the internet and memes.

So yes, big stuff – Challenger explosion, terrorist attacks of 9/11, the pandemic.

However, we fail to give the little stuff enough credit. All the small decisions we make – or even the ones we do not get to make – mold us into the people that we are today. Think about the second date you never had, the job you quit, the yellow light you didn't run that spared your life and you have no idea. How a few minutes, or even a fleeting moment in time, can alter our path completely. This is really cool when you think about the people you have encountered throughout your life and how some of them just keep reappearing. Or are in close proximity, but you aren't even aware as your lives are being lived completely parallel.

This reminds me of that old Gwyneth Paltrow movie, *Sliding Doors*. The year would have been 1998. Man, I would have been eighteen that year. Obviously, I knew everything there was to know about life. Just like my eighteen-year-old daughter currently does. (Insert a big sigh and eye roll here.) If you have not seen it, I highly recommend it. It is insane to see what five minutes difference can do. She missed the subway and her whole path altered. It also has a killer song in it and it is stuck in my head now. "Have Fun, Go Mad" performed by Blair. It makes you want to bounce around in your seat. You Tube it. You'll see. Parents of teenagers, blast it about 7 AM on a Saturday.

This is totally going to be a thing as you are reading. I pretty much have a song playing in my head ALL the time. Non-stop. While having conversations with friends, while lecturing to students, while trying to reprimand my children. So, when one pops up – you are gonna hear about it – and you are gonna love it. Lots of genres. I like to consider myself a well-rounded girl. (You should see when someone asks me to pass the Salt-N-Pepa at supper.)

Write your big-ticket items in this box – seriously, do it – unless you borrowed this from a friend. I am a big believer in writing in books. Highlight, underline, write in the margins. Own your shit. Literally and figurately.

Now, let's take some time to reflect on the things that were not immediate big items, but turned out to be really important to the person you are/are becoming:

I Got a B in Statistics

Yep, ruined my 4.0. I hate math, but I do love statistics. The numerical data that gives us correlations and causation. No matter what happens to you, I can assure you with statistics you are not alone. Which is somewhat, oddly, comforting. From the moment you are born, the numerical data starts stacking up. You were such and such number baby born in that year. Women are two times more likely to be diagnosed with depression, fifty percent of marriages end in divorce, or one in four women will have an abortion.

We examine statistics often in my psychology and sociology courses. I like to root for the underdog and love stories that defy the odds. However, the ugly truth is a lot of real data lies in these numbers.

Public schools get funding based on test scores and statistics. Lower scores = less funding.

Children from divorced homes are more likely (statistically) to be juvenile delinquents, teenage parents or drop out of high school. Ok, this one personally drives me crazy and was the topic for my master's thesis. We will circle back.

Quick shout out to the dedication page - I have been preaching that statement to my daughters since they were little girls. Hollering that same lesson to every single one of you.

La, La, Labels

Cha, cha, Chia. Am I showing my age here? Chia Pet commercials and that damn song.

Labels are the ugly stepsister to statistics, in my humble opinion. These stack up on us as well, throughout our entire life. In fact, they are much more front and center - impacting your daily life more than statistics ever could. Not all labels are bad - (i.e., first cousin or your profession) but the interpretation and application of some labels can be harmful.

Maybe you were the 'bad' kid, or the 'fat' kid. The middle child, the short one, the hyper one. Labels are placed upon us by our families, teachers, friends, and ourselves. We have the tendency to live up to (or down to, depending on your perspective) the labels applied to us. Take a moment to think about all the labels that have been placed on you. I will share many of mine throughout this story.

Keep in mind that labels can appear to have a positive connotation - such as people pleaser or over achiever. However, these labels can become part of who we are at our core and can be really hard to live up to. Many times, people start to behave like the label that is being applied – even it if is a false one. Well, if they are gonna say I am bad, I might as well get into trouble. Husband is being accused of being a cheater, might as well do it anyway. I think you get the idea.

Sidenote: Chia Pets were invented in 1977. They are older than me and have stood the test of time. I am not sure this is relevant, but it is a fun fact and we all need more of those. According to Nelson Mandela, "Knowledge is the most powerful weapon you can use to change the world."

Write the labels that have been placed upon you in this box – think all the way back to your childhood until now:

Who the hell am I? And why should you keep reading?

Well, isn't that the lingering question for all of us? In a nutshell: professor, wife, mom, stepmom. Daughter – only child (keep your spoiled comments to yourself). Finally realizing what I want to be when I grow up at age thirty. Molding the minds of thousands – some future leaders – and probably some future criminals.

Finding faith – not religion – but in myself. Spirituality. Reigniting the light in my soul that at one   point . . . well, it had totally burnt out. Picking up the pieces of broken marriages. Of myself. Sobering up in a jail cell.

I am a believer of "name it to tame it". Gotta handle all the feels, to get through them. Laugh. Cry. Yell into a pillow. Pretty sure my favorite emotional check point is in the shower. Can you relate? A good ugly cry is best in the shower. Talking to yourself – pretending you are going off on the person you were too nice to say anything to before – also best in the shower.   Singing the worst/best 90's songs ever – you guessed it, the shower. You know exactly what I am talking about – don't try to front.

Dance it out - *Grey's Anatomy* fans picture Meredith and Christina. (Insert those old John Michael Montgomery lyrics here "life's a dance you learn as you go".) But, don't slip and fall. I am forty-two – if I had a broken hip . . . well . . . hell, might as well put me down like horse. <u>Lots</u> of negative energy has disappeared during my kitchen dance parties.

This is my story – based on my four decades of life – which is about two thousand weeks. Based on the premise we live to be 80, I am about half way through my time. I thought about turning this into a glass half full versus glass half empty moment. However, I am a realist and there is no glass. (I am actually really thirsty now that I think about it.) While I do not foresee this being a best seller or sitting on a stage with a talk show host, I do hope that by sharing my story I can help you find some inner peace. Make you laugh along the way. Possibly cry – I apologize for that part. Life will try to break you – and it is up to you to build yourself back up. I have learned support systems are great, but others cannot do the work for you. You have to get down in the trenches and fight for yourself.

Part One:
Just Getting Started

Eighties Baby

I was born on the day JR - the villain on the television show, *Dallas* - was shot. It was March 21, 1980. My mother has told me this story about a hundred times. I Googled just to confirm because you never know . . . parents and their weird stories.

I was supposed to be a boy. No ultrasounds for healthy pregnancies back in the day - so they just assumed. I was going to be Carl the Third. My room was already painted blue. I had a badass train set waiting for me. This would be the moment that the label of gender had already started impacting me - and I was not even born yet.

Surprise! I am a girl. Insert Label #2 - not the gender they anticipated. Carl quickly turned to Cristina Renea. (Just like having unique teeth, I had to have a unique name spelling, too. God bless my mother.)

Annnnnd, immediately another label - "only child". This has been one of the most horrible labels throughout my entire life and honestly, I do not know why. Only children are not all spoiled, antisocial or unable to share their stuff. In fact, if you actually look into the pilot research on only children that started this whole frenzy, you will see the data set was tiny and it is all a load of crap.

However, I would be the only child they would have – because my folks were 35 when I was born. That was pretty old for new parents in 1980. I became the center of attention – especially to my mother. Sitting here today, I do not think that has really changed. I will make fun of my parents – a lot – but I must disclose the truth upfront: they are two of the best human beings ever to exist. I was a good kid, but a shithead teenager and an adult full of poor choices. They have been in my corner throughout all of it.

I was bald until I was two. My mother put me in dresses and ruffled underwear. I was an only child, so I played pretend a lot. When my parents no longer wanted me to use a pacifier, my mother had me watch as my Kermit the Frog puppet ate it. That will fuck you up. Let me tell you. Hated frogs ever since. Just kidding – I don't even remember it – thank you, infantile amnesia. I had an imaginary friend named Brian. He had red hair. I sat on him and he died. Yeah, so there's that. So it begins . . . my issues with maintaining healthy relationships. The key is boundaries, people, boundaries.

Dallas was a television soap opera airing in the evenings. Viewers would have to wait months before who shot JR was revealed. *Dallas* had a spinoff show, *Knots Landing.* That was one of my all time favorites growing up.

Honestly, there is no way I could understand what I was watching at the time. But they all lived in a cul-de-sac and always had great hair. I loved it.

The Little People Pleaser

I had an amazing childhood. I never wished that I had brothers or sisters. I was pretty content doing my own thing. One of my best memories was playing school. I had a pretty cool fake classroom in our basement. I was always the teacher and the neighborhood kids would actually do the homework I assigned them. It is unreal what kids will do to earn a stupid sticker. Weird. Vivid memories of being teacher's pet at Yankee Ridge Elementary. I always felt like a champion when lining up on the space for Room 131 on the blacktop outside.

Oddly enough, I never wanted to be a teacher. It wouldn't even occur to me until much later in my life.

My parents never fought. My dad was a union pipefitter and my mom stayed home with me. I had the picture-perfect childhood that many kids dream about. I do not recall going without anything I really wanted – and definitely had everything I needed.

I believe my need to please everyone did stem from my childhood. I don't say this in a negative manner, but I was the only one. So, it was always me that had to get the best grades, read the most books (me, in kindergarten – I am sure my mom still has the tee shirt I was awarded, she is the keeper of all crap). It was always me if something was broken, too. Oops. "People pleaser" and "over achiever" are two labels that do an intricate dance together – like a country two-step – trying to not step on each other's toes.

Little did I know this was going to grow and grow into adulthood. These labels coined with anxiety can be crippling sometimes. I digress.

Fear

Think about the things that you are afraid of. Some of the most common fears are heights and snakes, fair enough.

What scares you? Anything – write them here:

Now think about those fears – were you born with them or did something happen to you to cause them?

My biggest fear is going under water. Yes, I bathe and shower. But I only doggie paddle in pools. My girls are like little mermaids, so obviously this fear was not passed on. My fear stems from the two times that I was completely ignorant and sat under water in pools. Thinking you are going to drown a couple times will seal your fate, lemme tell ya. The first time it happened I was in the neighbors' pool. The raft docked on the side of the deep end. I should have been smart enough to step out of the boat onto the deck. Nope, I decided to step off into the water. I sank. I sat there. It felt like a lifetime. I finally started coming up to the top as my dad was jumping in to get me. What a moron.

The next time I was at the public pool. I loved going to this pool because it was the 1980's and you sewed your metal pool pass onto your swimsuit. They had the best candy, too. Anyway. I was sitting on the stairs with some boy – the son of some lady my mom knew. He was older and taller than me. He kept sitting on the steps showing me the water did not go over his head. I was afraid, but followed his lead. Next thing I know, I am sitting on the bottom of the pool. It felt like a lifetime (sound familiar, see above). Here comes mom to save me. What a mean boy. What a stupid girl. That was the end of going under water for me.

So, snakes, bugs, clowns, water, whatever. It is really a waste of space to examine fear without – at least for a moment – reflecting upon the other big things that scare you. Leaving a job, death, getting in a relationship.

Take a moment to think about the things you would like to accomplish – but you are afraid to do so. Write them here:

I have learned in my older years (cause late 30's and early 40's is like dinosaur age to many) that there are AMAZING things on the other side of fear. Fear can challenge you to soar to new heights. Fear can drive you to do incredible things. If you do not let fear own you, you have the power to completely change for your life. Fear is just a reason to try harder.

comes mom to save me. What a mean boy. What a stupid girl. That was the end of going under water for me.

So, snakes, bugs, clowns, water, whatever. It is really a waste of space to examine fear without – at least for a moment – reflecting upon the other big things that scare you. Leaving a job, death, getting in a relationship.

Take a moment to think about the things you would like to accomplish – but you are afraid to do so. Write them here:

I have learned in my older years (cause late 30's and early 40's is like dinosaur age to many) that there are AMAZING things on the other side of fear. Fear can challenge you to soar to new heights. Fear can drive you to do incredible things. If you do not let fear own you, you have the power to completely change for your life. Fear is just a reason to try harder.

Wanna See My Pussy?

Every kid does dumb stuff and has the stories that will just never die. Here is one of mine. It was my fourth-grade year. I was hosting a *Clue* party. Not like sit and play the board game, but my whole house became the actual playing board. I was Miss Scarlet and I wore a poofy red skirt and some big dumb feather headband. There are photos somewhere – again, thankful I grew up prior to social media. How embarrassing. Each room was a room on the board, my friends all came dressed in character and we rolled humongous dice to make our moves. It was fun.

When we were all done playing, I wanted to show my friends our two cats that lived in our basement. I yelled much to my dismay, "who wants to see my pussy?" and took off down the steps. I remember boys following me and them laughing. I wasn't even as many years old as I had fingers. I was naïve. Sheltered. So, there's that.

I found the photo. I cropped out the others to spare them the embarrassment. I am not sure which is bigger, the feather headband or my two front teeth.

My cats were Duchess and Whiskers – they were white and I got to pick them myself from my Uncle Jim's barn. Sorry to anyone who was disappointed about my pussy(ies), but I adored them. Hairy. Snuggly. Horribly allergic to cats.

If this was not embarrassing enough, fourth grade would also be the year that the first boy would ask me out. He called me on the phone. A landline with an actual cord. He asked me if I wanted to "go with him". I was confused and kept asking where he wanted to go. He finally got frustrated and hung up on me. Thus begins my innate ability to maintain a long-term relationship.

Tell me some of the dumbest/most embarrassing things you did as a kid:

I Wasn't Crying Wolf

My first experience with domestic violence would happen when I was about seven or eight years old. I didn't realize that is what I was witnessing at the time. Our house had a gorgeous big bay window that looked onto our street. I was looking outside one day and there was a woman on the hood of a car – as the car was starting and stopping driving down the road. She was screaming. I yelled to my parents, who didn't believe me. I am not sure why they didn't come running, I can assure you I was not a liar. I had plenty of other things to do than spend my time making up stories like that. I mean, I was a busy girl with my pretend school and vet office – plus my Cat Club craft sales in the driveway. (People will buy literally anything from a kid for a quarter).

Would you believe my mother still had this sign in 2022? Ancient proof that the Cat Club driveway sales did exist.

Anyway, the neighbor man started chasing the car down the road until the driver finally stopped. My dad went out to assist.

As it turns out, the couple was getting a divorce. The wife was on the hood of the car to try to stop the husband from taking their baby that was buckled in the backseat. This was not traumatic for me – but I cannot even begin to imagine what is like for children who grow up seeing things like this in their own homes. Every child deserves to feel loved, be cared for and to be safe.

For the first decade plus of my life, I thought my parents had been together forever. They got married when they were twenty-five, so I guess I just assumed. I would accidentally learn from my aunt that my mother had been married prior. Her first husband was physically abusive. This was the moment that I really started to think about experiences of people other than my own. What if my mom had stayed with him? I would not have been me. I could have been the baby in the backseat and my mom could have been the lady on the hood.

I was about 12 or 13 when the secret slipped out. I also learned that my father had been married prior.

Honestly, I was really upset for a while. I don't recall being angry they kept it from me; parents don't have to tell their kids everything. I just remember being dumbfounded because they always appeared to be perfect. Nothing is perfect.

Let's leave some space for you to reflect on the things you found out about your parents (or any other loved one) that altered your perception of them – even if only temporarily.

Return to Sender

Some of my fondest childhood memories are traveling to Biloxi, Mississippi to visit my grandmother, Edith Alene. My father's biological mother passed away when he was eleven years old. My grandfather, Carl Senior, would later marry Edith and she would raise my father as her own. She was all I ever knew for this side of my extended family. My grandfather passed away a few years before I was born. My parents swear I am the reincarnation of him.

I grew up in the 1980's with my extended relatives living a thousand miles away. Most of our correspondence was through written letters (mailed, like with a postage stamp). Little did I know that Edith would keep all of my letters and we would find them when she passed away in 2000. What were some of her most prized possessions are now mine, again. These were the days that I went by Crissy and I wrote about the most absurd stuff. I told her about my cats and Barbie dolls, counted down the days until I would arrive, listed everything I was planning to pack and what I wanted to do while I was there. Every letter was a repeat of the one prior - with the only change being a decrease in arrival days.

The bond that children can have with their grandparents is indescribable and irreplaceable. I was so lucky that she chose to become part of our family waaaay back before I existed.   We traveled to Biloxi every year over Spring Break – which also happened to be my birthday. In first grade, I had the chicken pox. We loaded up and went anyway – my parents said I could itch at home or in the car. True. We would always stop at this little rundown shack of a store on the side of the road in the hills of Southern Mississippi. I would buy junk. It was the best junk. Pencils, stationary, rock candy, stickers and paper dolls. A cat made from pecan shells.

I found another hidden gem – the darn pecan cat. My parents like to joke that when the pass away, I will have a lot to sort though. That ain't no shit . . .

Every time we would arrive, my grandma would have a new Care Bear for me. She drove with both feet and always had expired food. She was hard of hearing and played *Days of Our Lives* way too loud. She was the best.

We would go to Fun Time U.S.A. at least once a day for miniature golf (often timed during my grandmother blasting *Days of Our Lives* to avoid losing our sanity). Marineland was also one of my favorites. I have such great childhood memories of the Gulf Coast. Most of which are just in my mind now; Hurricane Katrina would wipe out all of my favorite locations in 2005.

Biloxi will always be my special place. I would later take my children there for vacations. My husband and I would spend part of our honeymoon there. My daughters would eventually take their girlfriends as teenagers, just like I once had.

I wish that Edith would have been able to meet my girls. She passed away from cancer a few years before my girls were born. Did I mention, she was the best?

Reflect on some of your favorite grandparent memories. If not grandparents, then the elders in your family:

Pavlov and Jesus

From preschool through second grade, I attended a
private Lutheran school. It was small, sheltered, expensive
and hypocritical. We went to church during school and my
parents faithfully toted me to service on Sunday mornings.
It was the mid-1980's and corporal punishment was a thing.

In first grade, my teacher (who was also the
principal's wife) would pull our teeth out. If she caught you
wiggling it with your fingers, it was hers. We learned to use
our tongues. She was the same teacher that tied my friend to
her chair with a jump rope. My friend would wander the
classroom – apparently too much for the liking of the
teacher and got tied up - like hands hogtied behind her back.
It was one of those plastic blue and white bead-like jump
ropes. How is anyone supposed to do their work like that? I
did learn to stay in my chair and not wiggle my loose teeth.
Classical conditioning at its finest.

For a few years of my life, I had religion forced upon
me. I am not sure if my parents had a falling out with the
church, but they decided to put me in the local public grade
school with all the neighborhood kids. It was a big transition,
but glad it happened in third grade rather than adolescence.

After we left that church and school, religion was never really a thing for us anymore. I cannot speak of my parents' beliefs, but I do struggle with my faith in a higher power.

I guess I just think the best way to live is to be a good human. I mean, we all behave badly at some point – but you know what I'm saying here. I don't need to tithe weekly to do that. I don't need a sermon to guide me or inspire me on my journey. I cannot stand when people are complete pieces of crap on daily basis, pray on Sunday and think that makes it all okay. However, I strongly believe everyone should do what is best for them. I also believe no one should cram their beliefs (or lack thereof) down anyone else's throat.

Having taught many years in a private high school, I see two types: the kids following in the religious footsteps of the parents and the kids who don't believe at all and are being forced. I see more and more young adults in my traditional classroom veering away from organized religion. The general consensus seems to be to leave them alone as long as they are not bothering you – whether that be politics, religion or sexuality.

In second grade at this private school, I was racing my teacher across the blacktop from our classroom to the church. She tripped and busted her face. I left her laying there and kept running. I wanted to win the race. I did. Smoked her. Probably ran my way right into a special place in hell, too. It's fine.

What are your views on religion? How have they changed throughout your life? What do you foresee in the future? Ponder it:

Growing Up on My Block

Developmental psychologists will confirm that babies and children who have attachment issues can carry those with them for the rest of their lives.

We know that kids need positive role models.

We know that children from two parent homes are (statistically) more likely to succeed.

This is where I am one statistical conundrum. We could argue the nature versus nurture debate all day long. Are we products of our genetics or our environment? In my case, I had to learn every lesson the hard way. In most incidents, the hardest way possible. I also realized that being "smart" wasn't fun in the early 1990's and I wanted to be "cool". I didn't care what the reasons were. I wanted to be noticed.

Well, I got my wish . . . I was on a one-way train to nowhere . . . the hot mess express, per say . . . and I was the conductor. Looking back on twenty-five years of dating history, I can see where my train derailed. The choices I would make as a young teenager would pave the way for decades of intimate relationships and the disasters that came along with them.

That boy from fourth grade that called on the 'ole landline? Well, he would become my very first boyfriend years later. He lived down the street and around the corner. He was bad news and I was hooked. Hanging out with him represented a whole new world that I wanted to be a part of. This was the same kid that would stand out front of our grade school pretending to jack off at the cars driving by. He smoked Newport's and weed. He lost his virginity in like preschool (ok, slight exaggeration there) and he liked me. I was fifteen. Nothing would be the same.

Oh. My. Gawd.

Feel free to email me your worst adolescence photos. I won't judge you. I promise.

All Aboard the Chu-Chu Train

In the mid 1990's the Quad City DJ's had a hit song, "C'Mon 'N Ride the Train". If you are anywhere near my age, you now have it stuck in your mind. Anyhoo, I can't help but laugh that this song was such a big deal and I would alllll these years later relate it to the beginning of my own train derailment. That's beside the point . . .

Let's talk about music from your high school days – music is heavily linked to memory and emotion. List some of your favorite songs from your teenage years:

Do you still listen to anything on your list? My guess is yes.

Do some or all of these songs bring back a specific memory for you? My guess is also yes.

As any true over achiever can tell you, whatever it is you do, you have to do it epic. Whether that means the best, the highest standards, the fastest, whatever. I cannot blame the people that I started to hang around during my adolescence for my poor choices. I cannot blame my parents; they had taught me right from wrong. I mean, heck, they only had me to keep track of. The only person I can hold accountable is myself. That's a big pill to swallow and most teenagers choke on it. Like I did. Pretty sure I kept choking until I was in my late twenties.

That first boy was experienced in every way possible and I was a sheltered "good" girl. He would be everything from my first kiss to my first experiences with sex. He taught me how to roll a joint. He was everything I wanted to be, cool. What a crock. It was definitely the start of my one-way ticket to Loserville, but he does not get the braggin' rights. That's all on me.

I remember smoking pot for the first time on 4/20. Yes, a total cliché. I was barely fifteen years old, I thought it was stupid. But all the people I thought were cool were doing it and peer pressure is a real bitch. This was the start of a couple wasted years being a stoner.

My first sexual experiences were consensual, however, I guess it was a form of bribery. If you do this, then I will like you more. Or, do this and I think I could fall in love with you. Many of you reading have been in this exact situation. It is the stuff we fear our children – especially daughters, sorry not trying to sound sexist but they are the ones who can get pregnant – will fall for. I lost my virginity at age fifteen. I wanted to, I think. I wanted to be loved. I don't remember it being great or horrible. It was just a thing that I did.

I remember a few weeks afterwards my mother was in the bathroom curling my hair. She asked me when we had gone from boyfriend/girlfriend to lovers. Ok, that was fricking awkward. Pretty sure I got the deer in the headlight look and that was the end of the conversation. My mother was from an older generation. We did not talk about sex. We did not talk about my first period when I was 12. In fact, I had no idea what was happening to me and I hid my underwear. As a human sexuality professor, I hear lots of stories of young girls doing the exact same thing. Again, people find comfort in knowing other people have been in the same strange situations as them. Some things are best left unsaid, sure. But some things should be talked about. In fact, this made me raise my girls in a completely different manner. I wanted them to know what was happening to their bodies. I wanted them to know about consent and the dreaded viral STI's that you get to keep for life. I would like to think I have done an okay job with my girls. They are eighteen and sixteen at the time of finishing my writing. I am winning at this mom stuff. We need to do more talking and less stigmatizing – on **MANY** topics.

Ok, so I can't help but laugh remembering back to 12-year-old me hiding my underwear. I also put **FDS** on my armpits for weeks because I found it in the bathroom drawer and didn't know it was for your coochie pop. I mean, seriously, talk to your children about this stuff.

As much as I would love to say that boy and I lived happily ever after, the statistics were stacked against us. Much to his dismay, we broke up about six months later. I don't remember the details, but it was time to move onto my next bad boy. Don't just smoke the weed, let's get caught and be arrested for it.

Officer, It's Not My Jacket

I was sixteen years old. I told my parents I was going camping and they gave me permission. I do not know for the life of me why they would have thought I, of all people, was going camping. I had in the past year found makeup and hair dye. I was more on that path than sleeping in a bag with bugs crawling around me. Anyway, they bought it and I was out overnight.

My second boyfriend was honestly, a nerd like me, who wanted to be a badass, too. So, he got arrested for stupid stuff – stealing nuts and bolts when he had the money in his pocket. One of the first nights we hung out he tried to steal a bottle of liquor from the store and got caught. Stupid, really. But young love is pretty dumb. So are teenagers.

Anyway, we were out past legal curfew in our friends little Ford something. Tiny crappy car. We had been to Steak 'n Shake and were parked at closed gas station. I was munching on my cheese fries in the backseat. Up rolls a cop. Strange car, parked at a closed location, middle of the night. Again, dumb. We were all stoned. I had the weed in my coat pocket because – being the ride or die girl I was becoming – knew my boyfriend shouldn't get into any more trouble.

Long story short – busted me for curfew, possession and intent to deliver. The crappy little red car had some bags and scale in it – that I knew nothing about. When the officer searched my jacket – I told him the truth, it was not my coat. I did, indeed, borrow it from my father. So, he called my dad and asked him. Unfortunately, my dad didn't pretend he left dope in his pocket and I was hauled off to juvenile detention.

It was an Illini leather jacket – think back if you can to 1996 – it was the one with an orange leather sleeves and a blue wool midsection. It is now 2022 and my dad still has that coat. Like, really, why? But that is not the point. We joke about it when we see it in the closet now. However, that night when I got home – let me tell you it was no laughing matter.

I was on my way to superstar status at the high school. Not only am I (presumably) cool but now I am a badass criminal with a record. I had earned my newest label: "juvenile delinquent".

Certified F Bomb

As if I had not made my parents proud enough by this point in my adolescence, I decided to keep trying harder. In true over achiever fashion, I got really good at skipping school and not doing my homework. I fell really far behind. I lived in Saturday detention – let me assure you, it is nothing like *The Breakfast Club* leads you to believe. My P.E. class was right before my lunch period and attending it just seemed stupid. Double lunch hour, driving around blasting Biggie and Tupac was way more fun and didn't cause me to sweat profusely. I pretty much gave up on P.E. when I realized in junior high, I had to change clothes in a smelly room with a bunch of girls. Nope, no way. My principal was a decent enough woman but when she would sit me in her office to lecture me, her wig would slide down her forehead as she shook her finger. There was no way to keep a straight face. That didn't help the length of my detentions.

The truth is high school really sucked for me. Yes, I skipped school. But a lot more stuff went on than me just wanting to pretend to be cool. For those of you who remember when wind pants were the thing – one leg up, one leg down. Picture it. (Sicily, 1923 as Sophia in *The Golden Girls* would say). Urbana, Illinois 1996. My first day of freshman year I watched a boy stab another boy in the arm with a pair of scissors. I took a lot of crap from a group of pretty nasty girls. My car was keyed, my locker was vandalized, I was smacked around in a stairwell. Constant hateful slurs - the usual words: slut, whore, bitch, cunt, rich girl, spoiled brat. I didn't want to be at a place all day, every day that was full of people who hated me.

I love when my students reflect on their high school years with smiles and positive vibes. Mine was horrible. The good friends I had growing up didn't want to hang out with me because I left them in the lurch trying to ditch the Crissy days. The group I put myself into was not the best choice. The boys were fine, I liked running with them because I liked working on cars and stereo systems. But a girl who runs with boys gets a bad name for herself - especially with the girls that want to date those boys.

It got to the point where I was not going to be able to graduate with my class due to absences and missed work. I had dug myself a hole that I was not able to dig out of. Let's add another label to the list: "high school dropout". The statistics looming around people who drop out of high school are staggering. And, in my opinion, irritating. This is not where life just stops. Sure, there are people who quit high school and live the rest of their lives working. So be it if that is their choice.

I am the product of a **GED**.

I say that proudly.

And it shocks the hell out of my students. They cannot believe that their award-winning professor is a "drop out". This is exactly the point I am trying to make – labels do not have to define you – unless you allow them to do so.

Some labels are harder than others to overcome, but anything worth having is worth working hard to achieve. I share this portion of my journey because I know there are students sitting in my classroom in the exact same situation. They should not feel inferior to their peers.

Upon my departure from my local high school, I wrote a letter to the Regional Office of Education asking permission to take my **GED**. This was before my class actually graduated.

They told me no.

I wrote them again. I persisted.

They said yes.

It is really odd to think that my over achieving self – who had become a temporary waste of space in the world – had brought it all back around.

If only things would stay that way.

I would enroll in my local community college with absolutely no idea what I wanted to do in my life. This happens – often. No plans, changed plans . . . it's fine. I see so many students being hard on themselves that things are going to take an extra semester. That they change their major . . . once or twice. (Heck, nowadays, students have meltdowns over missing a point on an exam – but that's irrelevant.) The pressure that people put on themselves is outrageous. I get it. I do it, too.

I started my college career in 1998 and finished graduate school in 2013. What should have been six years took fifteen. Life happens and that is quite alright.

In the most perfect full circle story of my life, I would eventually get my associates degree from that good 'ole community college. A couple decades later, I would return there as a professor. I love that story. My story.

Public Penises

There have been two times in my life that I specifically recall seeing men having their penises displayed publicly in stores for shoppers to view. Has this ever happened to you? Or do I just have the misfortune of these awkward moments? In case you have missed out, I feel that I should share my experiences with you.

The first time was when I was a young girl shopping with my friend and her mom. I believe the store was called Venture and I do know 100% that I bought some cassette singles this very day. Remember those? I still have a few – specifically my New Kids on the Block ones – but that is not important to this story. My friend and I had wandered off from her mother and were in the toy aisle. There was a man with his penis sticking out of the front of his pants. I remember my friend telling me what it was. I told her no, it was just the tag on his pants. Yeah, okay, Cristina. We took off to find her mom. I could not make this shit up if I tried. As an adult, I have to look back and wonder if he was a creep, confused, or what. So many people are irritated about the topic of gender-neutral bathrooms nowadays. These stories are proof you don't have to be in a bathroom to see someone else's genitals. Gimme a break.

The other time was in the juniors' department of a store at our local mall. I would have been in my early twenties. A man was standing near a rack of clothing, pants around his ankles, masturbating. By this time in my life, I would not be deceived this was a tag on his pants or that he was playing with his zipper. My friend and I went to tell the cashier and he ran out of the store - tripping and trying to pull his pants up the entire way. The store employee told me this happens often. Like really? Again, older and a little wiser now about fetishes and disorders - but super strange to accidentally view. I was just trying to buy a new blouse. Solid reminder to wash everything you ever purchase before wearing it. Yikes.

I wrote the penis section and for whatever reason I recalled another story later that evening when I doing dishes and singing to Frankie Vallie and the Four Seasons. It was the one time I accidentally saw a woman's vulva (not vagina - that's internal and an often-misused term.) I was at the Kentucky Derby with thousands of people in the infield - this area is known as party central and much cheaper than actual seats. I don't really know for sure - but I will say Mint Juleps do not taste great to me. Anyway, she was wearing a dress and had her legs spread open laying on a hill. All of these stories are equally odd - you know, when you are seeing something that is just not quite what you expect to be seeing – and it takes you a few moments to figure it out?

Yep.

This also leads me to think about the crack in between the bathroom stalls in women's bathrooms. Don't get me wrong, I am thankful for the door – but I think something needs to be done about the awkward space in between. Is this another version of America's crack problem?

It should be mentioned that the worst of the worst is when you are wearing a one-piece jumper thing (what's the actual name?) with a zipper in the back. You are basically sitting nude on the throne, praying that no one can see through the crack.

Briefly Reflecting on Just Getting Started:

This portion spanned nearly two decades of my life. But truthfully – all that time, I really was – as titled – just getting started. I had no idea what being an 'adult' had planned for me. No matter what your expectations are - you never really know where you will end up. Regardless, I was pedal to the metal towards . . .

Part Two:
Life in the Fast Lane

Queen of Homer

During the time I was floundering around in
community college, I moved out of my parents' house. I
bought a small place with a couple acres and a barn for my
horse. It was my little piece of paradise in little town called
Homer.

Looking back, I wish I had stayed home longer.
Home life was good, but I was ready to go – or so I thought.
Don't we all believe we know it all at this age? I loaded up
my stuff, my dog, my truck and the horse I was boarding and
forged on my path of adulthood.

Being an only child, I was used to entertaining
myself. Now I was out in the middle of nowhere, all alone. I
still had the nagging desire to belong to a group of people
that I had not exactly found in high school. My house

became the party house. Bonfires, fishing in the dark, all night booze fests, trying to not get decapitated as the horse ran its riders into the barn without warning. I do have lots of fun memories during this time period – but nothing that really matters. You know what I mean? It was just something to do.

I feel like I have lots of periods of my life like this. I was there. It was fine. But it was not me digging into the root of who I really was. Still trying to just exist.

I stopped smoking pot when I got arrested in high school and have never experimented with any other drug. I did not start drinking heavily until the month before my twenty-first birthday. Many nights I would go to bed while the crew was partying all night in my yard. I would clean up their messes and do it all over again the next day.

Even though I would not be the life of the party quite yet, I would eventually find a love for rum and line dancing. I found an escape from feeling anything and avoided everything. As soon as I was old enough to get served at the local country bar, the trouble would really start. The Queen was about to lose her crown and be dethroned.

The Queen of Homer was a nickname I had at the time – pretty sure I have the sash from the Halloween costume somewhere. Probably time to purge the basement.

Or ask my mother.

Where is the M&M Car?

It was Memorial Weekend 2001 and I had been invited to go to the Indy 500 with a friend – he got free tickets. I went. It was loud. I waited a really long time before asking "Where is the M&M car?" Evidently, that's NASCAR. I was at the wrong race. I only knew about the M&M car from playing the racing game on my Play Station anyway.

Fortunately, the race track had great hot dogs. Fun fact: race car is spelled the same backwards and forwards. That's a palindrome – like mom, boob and poop. Race car is probably the best one though because people won't believe you. They have to stop and think about it – which is fun to watch.

This day had no impact on my life.

It's just funny.

Sometimes we need to stop and laugh at the ridiculous stuff.

You Have the Right to Remain Silent. Please Use It.

It was a turquoise Chevrolet dually. I had a horse trailer to match. I would like to think I was the shit. Eh.

On the night of November 10, 2002, I would receive another label: "drunk driver". I was twenty-two years old. I am sure many of you have consumed alcohol and operated a vehicle, so by definition you are a drunk driver. However, being labeled in the eyes of the law is a different level.

We talk about this in my deviant behavior courses – are you a criminal if you break the law – or only if you get caught? If you really want to take a risk, use the next box to write all the times you have broken the law – any law, no matter how small. Yes, speeding and rolling through stop signs count. We are all criminals, technically. I just got caught.

Prior to this night, I had already had many close calls with my drinking. I remember speeding down the interstate coming home from the bar and a deer was standing in the center of the highway. That was not nearly as terrifying as blacking out and waking up as I drove through my parents' neighbors front yard. I came back to reality as my car was about to hit a large boulder right in front of their porch. I recall getting myself down the street to my folks' basement to sleep it off. The next morning, I went to work still drunk. A coworker noticed and drove me home.

The truth is, I needed that DUI. I needed a wakeup call. I was definitely out of control. I have wondered in the past couple of decades since this all happened, why no one ever tried to talk to me about my drinking. It is one thing to be hammered at home, it is another to get on the interstate going the wrong direction. I could have killed someone. (Yes, this really happened as well.)

On the night of my arrest, my friend asked for the keys when we walked out of the bar. I refused to give them to her – I specifically recall saying "Nobody drives my truck!". (Insert some deep-toned country gruff man voice here. It was obnoxious and would become my famous last words.) We left and headed to a party at a country house that was on my way home. This was right around the time that Nextel phones had come out with that neat-o walkie talkie feature (think back to 2002).

The phone was sitting on the center console as I was flying down a country road. When it squawked, I leaned right to grab it – when I leaned, I swerved – excessively. I wiped out a mailbox, stop ahead and stop sign. A portion of my wheel well was left in the yard. Bright turquoise. I kept going to the party – down the road and around the corner. I remember the people there helping hide my truck in a cornfield. A little while later the police arrived. As luck would have it, the lady who's mailbox I wiped out was in her front yard smoking at 1 AM and saw the whole thing. Smoking is very dangerous to your health and I do not recommend it. Save your lungs! So is drinking and driving. Don't do that either.

I bombed all the sobriety tests. The straight line was rigged. They asked me to pivot, I don't know what that means – but I did not ask for an explanation using nice language. I was wearing a god-awful cheetah print coat with faux fur from Hot Topic. I looked like trash, but this was the trend, I suppose. They questioned me about the black leather spiked collar in my truck. It was my dog's, I swear, I had many at the time. I was too drunk at the time to realize this was one of the lowest moments of my life.

A couple of years ago when preparing a lecture and drafting portions of this book, I attempted to get my original mugshot from the county. It has been removed from their system. It would have been really eye opening to see it after all this time.

I was hauled off to jail, talking about lord only knows what the entire way. My friend met me there with bail money and we went out to breakfast. Yep, straight from jail to scrambled eggs. I had to sober up, I had a wedding to be in that day.

At the time of writing this, the couple whose wedding I was in that day are still together. Never would have saw that one coming, but kudos to them.

During the time I was finishing up writing this book, my daughters and I drove past the local jail. They know everything about their mom – I have done this intentionally. If they learn from my mistakes because I am forthright, it is worth the scrutiny. One of them said how terrified they would be to be arrested and asked if I was scared when it happened. I was again, honest. No. I was not afraid. I was drunk and didn't have a care in the world. That is truly terrifying.

Friends in Low Places

One thing that keeps running through my mind as I share my life story with you is the importance of a solid, positive support group. We use the term 'friend' pretty passively. I mean the people who are really there for you – in your corner – no matter what. The ones that will call you out on your crap – even when it makes you angry.

Good friends are hard to find and they are even harder to keep. I can look back and see the exact moment where I left behind my 'people' for a new crew. That choice would propel me into years of being around those who brought out the worst in me. (Fact: friends should bring out the best in you.) However, it is really easy to find people who want to party – any day, any time.

There is also a huge difference in being alone and being lonely. I was used to being alone – but lonely was a whole new feeling to me at this stage of my life. I didn't know anything about who I really was. I didn't want to. I didn't like her and to this day, I don't know why.

I have told my daughters - who will be moving out eventually, before you leave this house – make sure you are comfortable in your own skin. As a young adult, I was not at all. I was one poor choice after another. Make sure you find comfort in solitary time – do not run from it. All I did was run for years. From feelings, people and problems. I wore out the soles of lots of fabulous shoes, running away from myself.

Two Little Lines

I was in the highlight of my career of being a drunken platinum blonde idiot. I showed up for my job that paid the bills, but by no means was a career. I was kinda dating a pretty nice guy, when I bothered to pay attention to him. I showed up at the local country bar. That is about all I did for what felt like an eternity. The DUI did not stop me from drinking, it just made me wise enough to stop driving. I was perfectly content with my horse and my dog, having children was not on my radar. Like ever. I was on a sinking ship with no emergency flairs.

My boobs were hurting – finally that growth spurt I had waited for since I was 13. Wooooo hoooooo!

I am tired all the time – hangovers will do that to you.

I feel sick every time I eat. Must be a stomach bug. Yeah, bug alright – called embryo.

I remember the moment I took the at home pregnancy test and those little lines showed up. My exact reaction was quite literally saying, "Oh, shit". I had recently gotten off the Depo-Provera shot and had been told by my physician that it would takes many months to get pregnant.

False. I know when it happened – precisely when it happened – I was merely a week out of jail for my DUI arrest. I was 22 with the mentality of a 17-year-old on a good day. What the fuck am I going to do now?

Sober up. Grow up. Oh my God, I have to tell my parents. Just a few weeks ago I showed up at their house fresh out of a jail cell. I am dead meat. Maybe I should just send an email about it. This is when I needed siblings, someone to be a bigger screw up and take the heat off of me.

My daughters are both fully aware that motherhood was not in my master plan. No one needs to read this and think I am an awful person for expressing these feelings in writing. The two best things that ever happened to me in my life were not my master plan – and that's okay: my daughters and my career. My daughter will joke that she's an accident. I call bullshit on her every time. She says it to get my goat. She was a surprise. I accredit her to saving me from myself, I sure wasn't able to do the job. If I had not ended up pregnant, I probably would have ended up dead.

The phrase 'get your goat' comes from horse racing and stealing the stabled goats that are there to comfort the race horses. Fun fact. Google it. You're welcome.

My Shotgun Wedding

I look like a cornered, terrified animal in the courthouse photos. I don't remember feeling that way, but the photo evidence is not so great. I was six months pregnant. Surprisingly, the rate of American women who get married during pregnancy is pretty high. So much for the cultural script I had always thought we had to follow.

A big wedding had been planned. I called it off. I didn't want to get married.

So here we are. At a courthouse. Doing something I did not feel was the best decision for me – but wanting to make everyone else happy. We would take some fake beach photos later, that will make it all better.

If I am doing what everyone wants me to do – it'll be fine. Right? I want to make this work. Ruben Studdard won *American Idol* the same day I got married. Yes, I remember really strange things. (I remember them without Facebook memories having to tell me stuff. That feature is a double-edged sword. I mean, sometimes, you don't want to remember everything.) I just looked him up because this made me wonder what ever happened to him. Not too much to report. Sorry, folks.

I had a few months to figure out how to be a mom. As always, I was clueless. Now I was clueless for the both of us.

Stay-at-Home Mom Blues

After being married for three months, I gave birth to my first daughter. She was named after my father since he got jipped when I was not born a boy as he had planned. Her middle name was in honor of my deceased paternal grandmother. Keep in mind, the entire time I was pregnant, I did not have a driver's license. I had to be a hauled for all my appointments, errands, etc. I did not get my license back until she was five months old. I had to attend my court ordered alcohol counseling classes while visibly pregnant. It was humiliating – especially since I was not pregnant at the time of my arrest.

Choices have consequences and it felt like I was doing everything the hard way.

A couple of years later, on 11/10/05 my second daughter was born. She was born three years to the day that I received my DUI. I, with one hundred percent certainty, believe that my children came into my life – when and how they did – to save me from myself. I needed purpose and they became my entire existence.

When Carleigh was born, she was in the NICU for a couple of days. I remember her shitting all over me without a diaper one of the first times I held her. Not the best start, but we seemed to have worked out the kinks since then.

When Camryn was born, the paging system in the hospital was not working and I nearly didn't get my epidural. Since before she was born, she marched to the beat of her own drum. She is currently sixteen and still doing so.

At the time, I was twenty-five years old with two small girls. I am a stay-at-home mom because I married someone who was able to pay our way. I am married because I got pregnant. I got pregnant because I was not responsible. Over my dead body would history repeat itself for my girls. It is incredibly hard to admit to people that you do not enjoy being home with your children 24/7. It is a life that many women can only dream about having. Tea parties, baby dolls, Barbies. It's also screaming, vomiting, sleeplessness, lack of time for yourself, lost sense of worth, and always something to clean. I was raised by a stay-at-home mother. I should be loving this. It was expected of me. I owed it to my girls.

I absolutely hated it.

Insert immeasurable amounts of guilt here.

Living up the expectations of others will kill you.

Trying to please everyone and make those around you happy all the time, will suck the life out of you. Regardless of your current age, heed my warning and stop doing this.

Amuse me. In this box, write what you have done for someone else this week:

I am guessing this box is full – or you even need more room.

Now, write what you have done for yourself this week:

Gonna guess that this box doesn't have much in it.

Childbirth is Basically Sexist Bullshit

I feel the need to lay it out here right now. Pregnancy basically sucks. It is super cool that a creature is growing inside you. Even cooler that they live in liquid and then shoot out and start breathing air. But, the public belief that pregnancy is great is a lie. I had things swollen that I did not even know existed prior. I lost my mucus plug on the bathroom floor. Thank God, I found it before the dog did. Probably wouldn't have hurt the dog, but may have caused me to gag watching her eat it.

Childbirth hurts like hell. I was thankful for drugs. I cannot for the life of me comprehend why anyone would want to do it naturally. I am not judging - do not get me wrong. Mad props to all the women who have done it drug free; in a field, on a plane, on a trapeze - whatever. It's just not for me. I am a pussy. My pussy is a pussy. (This is so politically incorrect, but I can't stop laughing. Sorry.)

New motherhood sucks a lot, too. I am pretty sure I got through the first week of my daughter's life by eating fistfuls of M & M's. I did, it was the mega jumbo ginormous bag from Sam's Club. Remember, I didn't have a driver's license so I had to stock up when I had a ride to the store.

More people need to express this openly. It's like all new moms are supposed to be magically good at it and love every minute. I did not. Why should I pretend it was all great?

This leads me back to one of my themes throughout this book - start talking, stop stigmatizing. There is always someone, somewhere who feels like you do.

Pregnancy was even harder the second time. My body was like fuck you, we are not doing this again. Ha! Jokes on you, this baby is going to scream non-stop for the first few months of her life.

Students in my lifespan development course (who have not given birth) freak out at the idea of pooping while in labor. Yep, it happens. Shit happens.

There have been two times in my life when I have shit the bed. Once was during the birth of my first daughter. The second was in the tanning bed. You don't even want to know.

I do love good poop stories – in your pants, on the floor, in bed, in a ditch, explosive children. Go:

If you really want to terrify your damn near (or already) sexually active children, Google images that compare cervical dilation to food items – like a pop can, cookie, etc. (Warning: you may never eat a bagel again). Then tell them it will never go back together. Follow up with some unpaid babysitting with no electronic devices allowed. Best birth control ever. You're welcome.

Broken Home

When my girls were four and nearly two years old, I filed for a divorce. This would be the first (of many to come) time labels were put onto my kids due to my choices. They were now going to be raised in a "broken home". I am not saying I agree with this label – in fact, I do not. Many children are better off from having divorced parents – and kids will tell you this. Statistically, however, they were now doomed. Stupid numbers. I would add another label for myself, too: "single mom".

I was miserable, I didn't try to do anything to improve the situation and I bailed. I bailed on my family. I was twenty-seven years old. I had not worked since I was pregnant with my first born. I was clueless of what I was going to do. This is a theme throughout my life. I did have, and still do at times the tendency to take big leaps without fully thinking through the long-term outcome. Compare this to the children's board game, *Candyland*. Instead of counting the color spaces and moving at a fair pace, I leap from the more eye appealing spaces such as the gumdrop, cookie or ice cream cone. This does not work. Let me assure you, I would spend the next decade of my life confirming: this does not work.

Another classic children's game that can be a great analogy for unhealthy relationships is *Chutes and Ladders*. I would not suggest that game as a lifestyle either. Again, lots of wasted time on confirming this, too.

My girls would grow up living in a house with me and packing a bag every other weekend to stay somewhere that was the polar opposite to the life they were accustom to. I would live with this guilt for a very long time. In fact, in some instances, I still do today. I would like to think that humans do the best they can in each situation they encounter. However, hindsight is always 20/20.

Many families struggle through the divorce process – drawn out, fighting, racking up attorney's fees. Mine took place is 28 days – similar to a detox program. I don't know that you can even wrap your head around a major life change in 28 days. It was calm, cordial and I received full-custody of my girls. I have always and will forever refer to them as my girls. I would spend the next two decades raising them to the best of my ability, on my own. They would become my two of my greatest accomplishments – even on the days I wanted to lock them in their closets. If you have parented teenagers, you can attest to this feeling. (No, I am not one of the *Dateline* families you watch about locking kids in their closets. Please do not call DCFS on me. Thank you.)

I remember after leaving the courthouse that fall day, stopping at a park. I sat on the bench alone and cried for what felt like hours. I had done what I wanted, so I am not sure what I was so upset about. While this was one of the biggest 'ticket' items in my life, I do not remember much else about it.

Everything had changed. As it continually does...

I needed a job. I needed to heal. I needed to process what my family had just endured.

Looking back, my best advice to young adults is to learn the art of pause. Pause before you speak. Pause before you leap. In true Cristina fashion, I would go from the frying pan into the fire.

The Best of Both Worlds

Yes, please, insert your Hannah Montana voice here. It was intentional. There was absolutely nothing broken about my house. My girls and I were thriving. I got a job that paid really well, they started preschool and life was good. Every night was kitchen dance parties, bubble baths with ice cream floating on boogie boards, and coloring books in my big king size bed. I was finally a happy mom and my girls were benefitting from that. My parents (because again, they are amazing) babysat and chauffeured. It takes a village and we were doing it together. Road trips, concerts, sporting events. My adventures with my girls are the best times of my life. I will forever cherish them.

They fought a lot.

I forgot my little one in the van once. She was only alone in the minivan for less than twenty seconds, beating on the window, yelling "Mom!". I still hear about 'how I left her' to this day. Cause she was the 'second born, not favorite child'. Give me a break. It was a very public place, someone would have found her, eventually.

We stayed in some sketchy motels, one of them stored their boogers hidden behind a canopy on the wall, we got peed on by a homeless man on an overpass.

They were best friends and worst enemies all rolled into one. I don't get it – siblings are weird. Like how can they be pulling each other's pig tails and then snuggling on the couch an hour later?

The one thing I was not mentally prepared for was the weekends they would pack up and leave. Friday nights to Sunday nights proved to be the longest 48 hours – every other weekend – ever. While it was nice to have a bit of a break, I did not know how to not be their mom and I needed to find something to fill my time. Most of my friends were happily married. I felt alone and lonely – again – and we know this can be a dangerous combination. Flip on the burner and bring out the frying pan . . .

I stumbled on this photo when digging through files for this book. I remember it being one of the best days ever. We spent the day in the pool. When it started to rain, we went skinny dipping. Afterwards, a beautiful rainbow appeared. When I first saw the photo, I hated it because I didn't have makeup on. We think about really silly, insignificant things sometimes. I guarantee the kids didn't give a crap about that – neither do I, now.

If you have children – write some of your best memories/traditions with them in the following box. We are reminiscing together and it is important to think about the happy times. If you don't have children, write about the best memories from your childhood – a tree gave its life for you to have use of these pieces of paper.

Strike the Match

I had broken apart my family for all about a minute before I started seeing someone. It all went down so quickly that it looked like I had been having an affair all along. I can assure you, that was not the case. I single handedly tore apart my family; I did not need an accomplice to do so.

I had known him since grade school. I feel like we had gone out a couple of times prior to my getting married. Yeah, yeah we did. I remember now. His house smelled like cat pee and it grossed me out. Anyway, I was 27 years old – freshly divorced with two children under the age of four. The fact that a man without "baggage" would be interested in me was flattering.

In case you don't pick up on them, there are themes developing here. 1) I think that I am not good enough; 2) I deserve the poor treatment I receive; 3) I do not stand up for myself even when I know what is right; and 4) I try to sell myself on fairy tales that do not exist.

Bachelors do not understand what it takes to raise small children.

Bachelors with insecurities do not understand that you have to speak to the father of your children – about the children – especially when they are such young ages.

Within a year of my divorce, I would be remarried. It was incredibly unhealthy. I don't even remember the date we got married – I repressed a lot from this time period.

He drank too much. He had a gambling addiction. He had mental health issues. He was a trainwreck. I wanted to help him. Cristina, the "fixer".

I recall a night in a St. Louis bar when I got smacked across the face.

He would show up at my house all hours of the night pounding on the door, drunk.

I woke up to a glass of ice water (with cubes) being thrown in my face to the words, "Bitch, wake up!"

He would get on the telephone while I was talking to my mom and tell her she was not allowed to come to my house anymore.

I began working as a secretary in a construction trailer. He hated me being around men. He called repeatedly to check up on me.

He was in severe gambling and tax debt. He would demand I change my will and leave my home and money to him - leaving my children with nothing.

My oldest daughter would hold my hair back while I vomited from panic attacks.

The list is endless. I don't want to remember it all.

I did not want more children. I made that clear.

He wanted children. He kept making that clear.

We would do the back and forth - work it out, split up thing - for what felt like years. In reality it was only a few months. It was one of a few very turbulent times in my life.

We would divorce. It only took 11 days. If you cannot tell, when I am done - I am done.

Ends up he had impregnated someone else while we were together. I guess we both got our happily ever after.

One in Four

I was only a few months freshly divorced from the father of my children. I would quickly dive into a second marriage and it was not healthy. I did not want to be in a situation that I would be having this individual in my life permanently. I was 28 years old. I had goals for myself and dreams for my two girls, both under the age of five at the time. By my own admission, I had no justifiable reason to be as sexually irresponsible as I was. I was not on birth control. I was not using condoms. I was relying on the pull-out method, which is a myth. A big lie actually, worse than a myth. They say that ignorance is bliss. In this case, it was not bliss – it was more self-inflicted bullshit.

Statistically, one in four women will have an abortion in their lifetime.

You know someone who has had an abortion. Even if they have not told you about it.

Start talking and stop stigmatizing.

Stop judging the decisions of others.

Most women who choose to terminate their pregnancy already have children and do not think they can take care of another. Many are in relationships that are not healthy. Many live in poverty. A large number of women were on some other form of birth control that was not effective. Some have been the victim of rape.

Regardless, I have always believed in the right to choose. If abortion is made illegal or impossible by TRAP (Targeted Restrictions on Abortion Provider) laws, young girls and women will still seek them. Historically, women have lost their lives doing so. Let's not forget the powerful message in the iconic film, *Dirty Dancing*. Folding tables, metal coat hangers, knitting needles. Real life horror stories – all of which can be prevented.

I contemplated sharing this part of my journey in my memoir. Debated on it pretty hard. At the end of the day, I did the right thing for the children I already had. I did the right thing for myself.

I do not regret it for a single moment.

I most likely would not have been able to become the woman I am today.

I am not ashamed.

I am one in four.

As stated previously in this memoir, I would later become a sex education teacher. Many myths surrounding sexuality need to be addressed; the pull-out method being the top of the list. Additionally, you can get pregnant while breast-feeding. Douching after sex does not kill sperm, it drives them up further. The lack of proper sex education in our country is astounding. Adolescents need to be armed with the tools and information to prevent sexually transmitted infections and pregnancies. Can I also preach for a moment about the importance of teaching consent?! Many schools do not have updated materials, use proper terminology, or have educational programs at all. Abstinence only education is not effective. Kids want to learn these things and it is up to teach them.

I have been very open with my daughters about this decision. Again, start talking and stop stigmatizing. I would want them to believe they, too, have the right to decide what is best for themselves. My openness allows them to feel assured that I would be there for them no matter what.

Briefly Reflecting on Life in the Fast Lane:

So many life altering events happened during these years of my life. As I look back, it is challenging to soak them all in. I would move out of my childhood home and live on my own for the first time. I was arrested. I gave birth to both of my daughters and endured multiple failed marriages. It was only a little over a decade of calendar days. That's the strange thing about time. Some weeks drag on and the years continue to fly by. No matter what, you've got to . . .

Part Three:
Keep On Truckin'

Knowledge is Power

It was time to woman up. How was I going to raise two little girls to be amazing young women when I was still floundering around with my own life? I knew I hated being a stay-at-home mom, but I had no idea what I wanted to be when I grew up. I was nearly thirty years old. I has finished my associates degree – but had no idea where I wanted to go from there. Many people fall into this trap. We get placed on this social clock of what we are supposed to do – and how long it should take – how old we should be. Everyone has their own journey – in their own time. Lots of people go to school, get the degree and hate the job they worked so hard to obtain.

I enrolled at Eastern Illinois University and completed my bachelors in a year. When you fart around at community college for like ever (122 credits) sometimes it pays off. Still clueless what I wanted to do – so I kept going to school. Much to my surprise, I was accepted to graduate school. Even though I had no idea at the time, this was going to be the moment that would later pivot my entire existence.

What was probably an embarrassing moment for many, was the waters parting way - come to Jesus moment for myself. I was sitting in a grad class and it hit me like a ton of bricks. As many of my classmates were getting their asses reamed for failure to use proper APA formatting this far along in their college career – I was having a moment. (In their defense, APA is kinda weird and tricky. Too many italics and periods, but whatever. I had a perfect score, but that is beside the point.) There were two professors during my graduate program that forever impacted me. I would not be where I am today without them. THAT is who I wanted to be. I wanted to make a difference in the lives of others – be part of their journey. I wanted to be a college professor.

Don't I look excited?!?

I chose to write a master's thesis because I wanted to dig deeper into the statistics that were stacked against children from divorced homes. I dedicated my research to my daughters. I would later repeat this study with students at Richland Community College. The findings were the same: children from divorced homes reported higher levels of juvenile delinquency. As families continually change, I would like to gather data a third time and compare the results.

Death Is Inevitable

During my early-thirties, the entire older generation of my family passed away within a few months of each other. This included my aunt and my maternal grandparents. This was a very hard chapter of my life. Not just because I lost people that I loved, but the changes that trickled down within my family – especially for my mother. My father had buried his parents spread out over time. My mother had to do it all within a few days. She carries guilt about decisions leading up to their deaths. I wish I could carry this burden for her.

It is always hard to lose a loved one. Although, I feel that we are better (for lack of another word) equipped to handle deaths of the elderly. There is something different when it happens to younger people. No one should ever have to bury their child. I am not sure which is worse - watching someone you love pass slowly or be taken from you suddenly leaving you with no time to prepare.

During this time frame, we watched two of our loved one's rot away from dementia. That is a strong term, but I used it intentionally. That is exactly what this disease does to its victims. Over a few months, I watched my grandfather and my aunt waste away, mentally and physically. One thing

I am incredibly thankful for is that I was able to have last (even though I did not know it would be) conversations with each of them.

My grandfather had gotten really hard to talk to on the phone and my grandmother acted like a gatekeeper – not letting him talk. They lived in Florida so most of my relationship with my grandparents was phone calls and letter writing. By the grace of God, when I called the house that day, my grandmother was out getting her hair done. My grandfather's nurse let him get on the phone. It would be the last time I heard his voice.

My grandmother would pass away six months later – on 7/11. (This was the same date I had presented my master's thesis the year prior, I am really weird about date coincidences like this. Are you?) She had been hospitalized and released to a nursing home. She was set to go home the following day when she had breathing trouble. She had a do not resuscitate order and the staff followed her wishes. She would be reunited with my grandfather. My mother would never forgive herself for not getting her home sooner.

My last conversation with my Aunt Jo was in person. She thought she was a little girl and was petting her stuffed dog. She was lying in a hospital bed with pool noodles wrapped around the bars to keep her safe. She died within a couple days of my visit. She held on overnight until her favorite nurse arrived for the morning shift to take her last breath.

Another strange thing about death is how people behave afterwards. I have vivid memories being a small girl when my great-grandmother died. After the funeral, I watched my uncle literally tag the furniture he wanted to get. Jewelry went missing. Family members would stop speaking for years. How people behave in life and death is fascinating. Humans are odd creatures. We are the only species who know we are going to die. How much does this alter our behavior on how we live?

I have always wanted to keep strange things – I have the clothes my grandparents were wearing in their last photos with my daughters. I also wanted their perfume and cologne bottles. Our sense of smell is very heavily linked to our memory. I can smell them anytime I want. She wore Estee Lauder Beautiful and he wore Old Spice. Sometimes when I just need to hit the reset button, I drag them out of the drawer.

Death is a thief. It steals the ones we love. It is best friends with grief. Grief is also a thief. It steals the lives of the living. I hate them both.

In my lifespan development courses, I ask students how they want to live their dash. They usually look puzzled. Picture a headstone with your name, the year you were born and the year you passed away. The dash represents everything in between. Your lifetime. How do you want to live your dash? What are some things you want to accomplish? What is the legacy you wish to leave behind?

Teaching Is My Jam

I received my first teaching job straight out of graduate school. I would drive nearly an hour each way, everyday - for really crappy pay. In fact, I am pretty sure I taught for free that first semester when you break down the time I spent commuting, prepping, teaching and grading. I didn't care though because I was finally doing something I was passionate about. That makes all the difference. When you find something that you honestly love doing, the whole world shifts.

My first class had eight people in it. I was a nervous wreck. Definitely sweated through the armpits of my dress and said "um" a lot. It's fine. This college took a chance on me when I was fresh out of school. I remember being hired the day before Thanksgiving – for the spring term. I was handed the textbook and master syllabus and told "good luck". I didn't stay there long, but I will always be incredibly thankful for them giving me a chance to make something of myself and pursue my dreams.

Over the years, I have worked for many institutions. I have had traditional and non-traditional students. I have taught online and face-to-face. I have been thrown to teaching from home and been cyberattacked. I have worked for private and public universities, community colleges and high schools. Every single student brings something different to the table. Maybe they are the one that snores in the back of the class – or maybe they are destined to change the world. Eh, you never know. I have loved every moment I have shared with my students – well, mostly – and the permanent impact they have made on me.

I read once that teachers should never say they learn from their students. What a crock. We are – regardless of your job, trade, or profession – always learning from each other. Isn't that the whole point? I feel that it is very narrow minded to assume we can only learn from specific people and settings.

Over the years my students have ranged from ages 16 to 76. They have been from all around the world.

My eldest student set a goal to graduate when she is 80, "if she isn't dead" and I am invited to her commencement. I told her I would be there with my air horn. Her knowledge and input were enlightening because she actually lived through many decades and remembers things that most of us can only read about. Honestly, it was really fun to watch her challenge the ideas of the traditional age students. I give her credit for returning to school at this point of life. I can only hope I am so on-it in my elderly years.

My youngest student received her associate's degree at the same time she graduated high school. She went on to receive her bachelor's degree and is starting graduate school at the age of 20. She mailed me the sweetest card the other day. I kept it to remind me on days that I feel useless that I do make a difference. (Self-doubt can really suck.)

The power of human connection is amazing.

The difference you can make in the lives of others is incredible. You may not even realize you impacted them but they will always remember you.

I challenge you to each and every day, be your best self. That version of you will change – some days are harder than others. Go to bed every night knowing you did the best you could that day – then let that day go. Find comfort in knowing that the following morning will be an opportunity to try again.

My student stories are endless. I have met countless remarkable people in my decade teaching college. Honestly, that will be another book of its own. They deserve more than just a chapter.

One Date Wonders

After my train wreck of a second marriage, I stayed single for a very long time. I did date occasionally. When I say date, I chuckle because most of my experiences were downright pathetic. I used to have the belief that I could handle a free dinner with just about anyone. This time period was definitely proof of that.

One guy showed up with his arm in a sling from the fight he got into the night before. The fight was over his girlfriend. When we went to the restroom, he could not zip his own pants. Not my problem. Strike one.

Another guy seemed to have it together until he started talking about when his teenage daughter would spend weekends and how they would sleep together and snuggle. He also had no driver's license. Strike two.

My favorite was probably the man who took a call from his daughter during our meal. He baby talked her so badly it made my ears bleed. Thank goodness we were at Texas Roadhouse – I could use the rolls as ear muffs. Strike three. You're out.

Oh, and then there is the guy that within five minutes of meeting me had my whole next two weeks planned out with him. No way, dude.

I gave up. Better off cleaning the bathroom. Washing my hair. Folding my socks. Literally anything but this. (Insert Terri Clark's "Better Things to Do" lyrics.)

Better off taking dumb selfies with my daughters...

Lay it on me – worst dates ever:

Monsters Aren't Just Under the Bed

After the demise of my second marriage and healing from the wounds, it took me a really long time to finally allow someone into my life and into the lives of my children. I had tried online dating – it sucked – great for those that it works out for. I know it can be a wonderful tool nowadays, but for me – it was a waste of time. I was afraid to meet a stranger and the idea of getting to know someone brand new was overwhelming. The one date wonders listed prior says it all.

One day a former middle school classmate reached out to me on social media. He was someone I had forgotten all about. He started messaging me – and relentlessly tried to take me on a date. After a couple of weeks, I gave in. I sold myself on the idea that this was not a stranger – he was an old friend – and in reality, that was total crap.

Even though I was very upfront with my intentions and rules regarding my daughters, I would quickly be intertwined into his narcissistic web. Quickly, I was breaking all the boundaries I had set in place. He was pushy, cruel and egotistical. This relationship lasted a little over a year. It escalated from psychological damage to physical. He never hit me – but he started to hit the walls and vehicles. He would throw things just close enough to scare me into whatever he wanted done. I was not allowed to use my last name on social media – which was my children's last name. I was forbidden to speak to their father. If I didn't answer text messages quickly enough, there were consequences. Threat after threat. If I didn't do this, then this would happen. Making it appear on social media that were this power couple as he tried to infiltrate every part of my life. He put a time stamp on when he had to move in or he was done with me. I was only allowed to have one night per week alone with my children – in my own home. I had to call and clear my every move with him.

Honestly, writing this now sounds really surreal. Although I have healed, the impact this time period had on the lives of my children was detrimental. They watched their mother go from a strong willed, independent woman to a puppet never able to perform perfectly.

During this year, I would lose a lot of weight. I was covered in a rash. I would physically tremble when he would come close to me suddenly or show up in my driveway unexpectedly. I had panic attacks. I can recall numerous times I would have to pull over on the way to class to vomit in the ditch.

Keep in mind, this man did not help me pay my bills. He was not the father of my children. He did not reside with me or have a key to my house. The power that he was able to have over me, when I gained literally nothing from the relationship, was unbelievable.

As he was constantly showing his true colors to me, I was constantly making excuses. I learned a lot of unfavorable things about this man during our time together from others – including domestic violence arrests, restraining orders, and a child emancipating herself from his care.

One day he was so out of control my girls went outside and called my parents. They showed up and threw him out of my house. He called immediately demanding I leave my children alone overnight and come to his place to show where I stood with my family. I did not go, but I did not stay home. I left the girls with my mother and checked into a hotel for the night. I needed time to think. I was in too deep and I was terrified.

We teach our children that monsters hide in their closets and under their beds. The reality is monsters climb into our beds – while our children are scared and crying across the hall.

Drowning with My Eyes Wide Open

It was a recurring dream. Nightmare is more like it. I am in lake and the water is pulling me under. I am fighting hard; my eyes are wide open; I want to get out of this. Every time I get my head above water, I can see a large hand pushing me back down. The hand has a very specific tattoo. I submerge under water over and over, gasping for each and every breath.

My house, my children, my self-esteem – all taken over by someone who claimed to love me. This "love" was going to kill me. I could not see a way out of this safely and I didn't think I could handle the pain I was going to feel if I exited the relationship. I was no longer myself. I wanted to die and I expressed this to people.

I am eternally thankful for the three things that would happen that caused me to keep fighting for those breaths.

The first was when I read my daughter's journal. I had never read it prior and have not touched it since – I swear. She would have been fourteen at the time. Old enough to be very articulate with her words. While I will not disclose everything, she wrote how much she wanted her mom back. How she missed the person I used to be. How she feared I was going to take my own life or be killed by him. The damage that had been done to my daughters by witnessing the domestic violence in their home – that was supposed to be their safe haven – would not easily go away. If ever.

The second was a photograph posted online of me – that I did not know had been taken. We live in a society where many of us take dozens of photos, photoshop and then post our favorite online. We pick out the world sees us. I grew up with cameras that had film, as perhaps did many of you – whole different playing field. If you want to see what you really look like, take a look at yourself in the photos where you are not perfectly posed.

I was at a graduation where photos of the audience were being taken and posted on Facebook. I stumbled on it a couple days later. This is the only photograph that I kept from this portion of my life. I saved it as a solid reminder of exactly what I would never allow to happen to myself again.

Although this may not look like a big deal to you, I was finally able to see what everyone was so worried about. It was the first time I was able to visualize the way I actually felt. My body language was so submissive – my facial expression looks like a scolded child. He is leaning in to reprimand me about lord knows what. I can guarantee I was saying I was sorry, even though I hadn't done anything wrong. All I ever wanted to do was keep the peace and avoid his threats becoming my reality. This was all I did for over a year.

Mercy, Literally and Figuratively

I knew I needed out. I was afraid of what would happen and I did not have any self-worth left to just be tough. Things were escalating quickly. I know the signs. For the first time in my life, I sought professional psychological help. I started talking – and talking – and talking.

This was the third item: Ironically, my therapist's name was Mercy. Yes, Mercy. In my journey to find the self-compassion I so desperately needed, I found it in literal form as well. I am a big believer in signs and all of this was adding up to big changes.

She confirmed everything I already knew – I was being abused. I teach this stuff. Why is it so hard to stand up for yourself when you already know what they are telling you as fact? I wish I knew the answer to that. I am sure many of us do. She and I worked together to build up my courage and to process what was happening to myself - and my daughters.

She told me I was strong.

I will never forget that or the look on her face when she said it.

For months I had felt weak. I had let a person take over my perfect world and destroy it. How could I be strong?

She said that because I was still maintaining my career, taking care of my children, and sought out help – I was strong. That was the turning point for me. It was time to change the narrative – I would no longer be the puppet. I needed to be the puppet master.

She said the best and safest plan was to let him think he was dumping me. Instead of begging for forgiveness for whatever ridiculousness I was always being accused of, just let him dump me. I waited – it took a few weeks. I knew it was going to be a hard habit to break – I was so trained to do what he wanted. But I was STRONG and I had MERCY. We were driving into town to return a pair of pants. I was driving and he started screaming at me. (This happened all the time.) My crossbody purse was half wrapped around me, half sitting by me in the seat. He ripped it off of me and threw it out the window. When he came across the seat, I remember thinking he was going to punch me. I remember thinking I am going to wreck the car on this curve.

I pulled over to collect my items from the side of the road. It is incredibly degrading to be climbing around in a ditch of tall grass to collect your bubble gum, maxi pads, and wallet. He decided he was so angry he was done with me. He wanted to go back to his car at my house and take the few items he had there. He kept bringing things for months, I never made a space for him. I didn't want his things there, but he just kept pushing.

I shook the whole way home. I was afraid to be alone in the car with him. I was afraid what was going to happen when we got back to the house. My girls were there. Was he really just going to leave?

Yes.

Yes, he did.

He came inside and collected the couple of items he had and sped off down the road. He immediately (and I do mean within a few minutes) went onto Facebook to announce he was 'single and ready to mingle'. He bashed me for being a crazy person and needing to 'take my meds'.

When a narcissist can no longer control you, they try to control the way the world views you.

I blocked him on everything.

I heard through the grapevine, he moved onto his next victim. With warp speed.

And I earned my next label, "domestic violence survivor".

Domestic violence comes in all shapes and forms. It does not have to be bruises and black eyes hidden by sunglasses. It can hide in plain sight. The damage from emotional and psychological abuse can be just as harmful as a smack or kick.

History Repeats Itself

As I sat here writing – drafting portions of my journey, not necessarily in order . . . I gave myself the "domestic violence survivor" label during the last relationship. Obviously, this was my second severely abusive relationship based on the behavior of my second spouse. I knew this – I have known this for years.

I guess I just never really stopped to put a label on it. My girls were so little at the time and I had to pick myself up off the floor – literally and figuratively – and carry on. I didn't have time to process it all.

I put my kids through this trauma twice. If there is anything I can say confidently, it is that they have learned exactly what not to do in relationships thanks to their mother.

I want better things for my girls that than the horrible choices I have made – and forced them into with my decisions. They have suffered incredibly.

The cycle of feeling unworthy needs to stop.

The feeling of needing to help others – who do nothing but harm you – needs to stop.

I didn't deserve any of this. Either time.

Neither did my daughters. Either time.

The night I wrote this section I laid awake in bed thinking. It is easy to see throughout my life my choices in relationships were not the best judgment. However, I have to question if I am more likely to keep putting myself into unhealthy situations due to my past. I question if this will subconsciously be woven into my children and their choices.

I wonder if my second abuser had an easier way into my world since I had been there before. It would make sense to think it would have been harder – that I would have run from the red flags – but maybe it is easier because we put ourselves into things that are familiar. Familiar, even when bad.

It would be disingenuous of me to present my lifetime of relationships as these two being the only unhealthy ones. It has become very clear to me over the past few years - unhealthy is what I know. Chaos. Whether it be big or small, it is what I am used to. I have repeatedly sought out individuals – or allowed them to pursue me – even when I knew in my gut it was a poor choice. This circles back to the four themes I mentioned prior: belief I am not good enough, acceptance of the poor treatment I receive, failure to stand up for myself, and wanting my fairytale.

In reality, most fairytales have unhealthy events – the mom dies, the stepmom sucks, or you have to clean up for a bunch of short guys. At this stage of my life, I think it is more about how we persevere on our own that makes us triumphant. It is not about a prince riding in on his horse to save the day. I can ride my own damn horse.

Our personal history of decisions and patterns become hard wired into the core of our existence. We seek feelings that we are used to. If these are positive ones, great. In many instances, at least in my lifetime, they have not been. This is an incredibly hard cycle to break.

Ghosted

It was not until the past couple of years that I have seen lots of research on the impact of being ghosted by your best friend. Everyone knows the text game - respond less, take longer in between when you are losing interest in a romantic partner or want to run someone off. Sure, whatever. I am not talking about the lousy blind date you want to avoid. I am referring to your absolute best friend vanishing on you. When this happened to me, I thought I was ridiculous for being so hurt. Strangely, I felt like expressing my feelings to other people about the situation would make them think I was nuts. It honestly felt like a break up. Even worse. But, why?

I have read some interesting articles lately about soul mates and the fact we put too much pressure on our romantic partners. That, perhaps, our best friend is our soulmate and that the person we marry fills a very different role. I think it really important to acknowledge the loss of a friendship – a true friendship stings. Let's not confuse intimacy with sexuality. Best friends are the ones that can read you like a book, who will clean up your kids' vomit, and who look out for you when you are too naïve to do it for yourself. You confide in them, you trust them. When they vanish on you, it leaves you with a gaping whole. This leads me to question if the level of friendship is completely subjective. While one person feels like this person is incredibly special, clearly the other one does not reciprocate.

I suppose this happens in relationships/marriages as well. It is a little alarming how people can just delete you out of their life – with no explanation – without looking back. Especially in an age of constant connection. Are we putting less effort into the relationships we have now than in the past? Do we value the importance of others less? If so, why?

If you have ever encountered something like this, I encourage you to drop your thoughts and feelings below. Maybe it was in your childhood or adult years. Doesn't matter – still hurts.

The Power of Words

Before finalizing the release of this book – I was talking to my oldest daughter about my writing. She thought I said "riding" so she asked if it was horses or penises. (I about peed my pants laughing and she gave me her blessing to share our story.)

When my younger daughter was five, Lady Gaga released a song called "Poker Face". She thought it was "poke her face". She would sing it and repeatedly poke me in the face. She also told me in third grade that a boy "hits her and spits on her everyday". I was pissed. Well, with a little more explanation, I learned he spits when he talks and he flails his arms around when he walks through an overcrowded classroom. Neither of these behaviors were intentional.

My older daughter has always been on me about my fashion sense – or lack thereof, in her opinion. She yelled from one end of the house, what I thought to be "Mom, can I use your cardigan?" Ummm, sure what color. You hate my sweaters. "Card again. Credit card."

Articulate your words the best you can, always. This is hard in face-to-face conversation, but even harder in an era of email and texting. I cannot count the times that I have had misunderstandings (sometimes big ones) though messaging. Words are generational and geographical. While they are just your mouth changing positions to form specific sounds, they can still be very harmful.

I remember in high school some girl (I know who but I won't rat her out here) wrote "Christina is a big stupid bitch" on my locker in pen with clear nail polish over it. One, she spelled my name wrong. Two, I was not big. Three, I was not stupid – that was an act. You would not believe how long it took a janitor to figure out to use nail polish remover. That was on my locker for weeks. Here is a good word for that guy: moron.

It was Ruth Bader Ginsberg who made the quote, "Speak the truth even when your voice shakes" more widespread. (It was Maggie Kuhn, founder of the Gray Panthers who originally said it in a longer version.) This is a motto I strive to live by, but can be really hard.

Tell me about sometimes you had to tell the truth
and were terrified to do so – big or small:

Briefly Reflecting on Keep on Truckin':

I would best summarize these years as when I finally had to grow up and face my demons. This section consisted of less than a decade but packed full for life changing events - good, bad, and everything in between. I carried on through many hardships which ultimately prepared me for . . .

\

Part Four:
The Long Haul

Third Times the Charm

When I started to write this portion of my story, I had it in the prior section - Keep on Truckin'. I already had decided what was going to be in this section - The Long Haul. I thought on it for a bit and decided it needed to be moved. This space seems way more fitting - I am going based on the assumption that third time's the charm - rather than three strikes you're out. (Self-fulfilling prophecy at work here, fingers crossed!)

After a few months of being blissfully single, I received a Facebook friend request from some cute guy sitting on a motorcycle - with big ears and an even bigger smile. We had lots of friends in common from all parts of my life, I accepted. Within a few minutes, a private message. His status on his page was single and my initial thought before reading the message was, here we go again. His message was cute, pretending the thought he had seen me around - blah, blah, blah. Nope, don't think so. He asked me out, I blew him off for a few days and then decided why not. I mean, I did used to have that dinner with anyone motto. I like food.

The truth is, I went digging through his Facebook page. It was the photo with his dog that convinced me. It wasn't some posed fake photo, it was him sitting on the floor being mauled by Black Lab kisses. (Her name is Sage and I now get this thrill of cleaning up her vomit and shaking her paw anytime she wants me to.)

I nearly bailed on our date. I didn't see the point in going.

He nearly bailed on our date because he thought I was going to be too smart and we wouldn't have anything to talk about. (Aww, how sweet.)

It was November and cold. I got to the restaurant first. I had noticed some dodo cruising around on his motorcycle. I specifically remember thinking how cold it was and how stupid I thought this guy was. Well, you guessed it, it was my date.

We sat at dinner for three hours. Talked about everything under the sun. Were adamant we were not looking for anything serious, just weekend dates when we each had time. (We have been inseparable ever since - glad we both played hard to get - but pretend you don't know that part yet.)

He texted me right after I left dinner. You know, the I had a great time tonight stuff. Sigh.

Wanna hang out tomorrow? No.

Next day? Sure. I agreed to breakfast. He can't be too much of a tool bag if he wants to meet for pancakes on a Sunday morning. I wore my ugliest, holiest (as in actual holes, not Jesus wannabe) overalls. I am not sure if I was trying to scare him off or was just like, yep this is me deal with it. Anyhoo, when I got there, he was sitting outside on his motorcycle – in the freezing cold. Good lord.

That was it. We went from being complete strangers to realizing over the coming weeks that we had been in the same place and the same time for two decades. Our parents all knew each other before we were born. Tons of friends (real friends, not social media friends) in common. Twenty years ago, when I worked at a bank, he was one of the muddy construction workers that would ruin our lobby every Friday. We hated these guys. When I was a teenager, I was at a lady's lake house – about fifty miles from home – it was his aunt. He grew up visiting that house and going out on the same boat. Small world, indeed.

Some of you are thinking it – the dreaded word: soulmates. No. Harsh no. I do not and never will believe in soulmates. However, I do believe that things are meant to happen in their own time. We both had two children, two failed marriages and multiple years of other failed relationships. We were both fully functioning adults, established in our careers. We did not need each other; we wanted each other – and that makes all the difference.

We would be married within a few months of our first date. It was a beautiful, small ceremony on his family's land on the hottest (like 115 degrees) day of the year. Our children were our attendants. Our reception would be at the place where we had our first date. I could not have asked for a more perfect day.

As much as I would love to tell you that we rode off into the sunset, happily ever after, that would be false. We met in the middle of our lives and that comes with some issues. We blended four children (this part was honestly really easy because they were all older). There were substance abuse and mental health problems, unacknowledged issues from our pasts, aging parent struggles, and the typical differences in opinion on the usual crap.

Our prior marriages were mostly out of obligation to our children. I am not saying the marriages were necessarily unwanted. However, they were somewhat of an expectation. This time was different. Even on the days we challenge each other more than we should – and trust me, these days occur – we still have each other's backs. We are a work in progress – isn't everyone?

Yet again, I am a "wife" and add a new label: "stepmom". I do not think I am the dreaded Disney stepmother – but I guess you would have to ask the two boys (young men) who got stuck with me.

We would be married a mere seven months before the whole world would shift.

For the only time in my life – except when my parents decided to make me an "only child" – I would get a label that I didn't inflict upon myself. This next one would be totally out of my control.

Falling into Madness

It was a Wednesday morning, February 26, 2020. I woke up feeling miserable. I wanted to cancel my classes, but I never cancel – so I showered. Exhausted, sitting on the side of the bed. I felt like I had been run over by a bus and I was having a hard time breathing. Holding onto hope that the snowstorm outside would be enough to shut down the two high schools expecting to see me that day. My prayers were answered, back to bed I went. I would be there for nearly two weeks, with no concept of time or what was truly happening to by body.

Across the globe a new, deadly virus referred to as Coronavirus (COVID-19) was rapidly on the rise. It had made its way into America – no one was quite certain when it had truly arrived.

For the first five days, I laid in bed and baked. My fever was nearly 104 degrees. I slept a lot and coughed a lot. I didn't eat much, but when I did there was no taste. This was not like when you are sick and your taste buds are off, this was different – no taste at all. My entire body was in incredible pain. I didn't have contact with many people during this time, but I do recall texting a colleague and expressing how bad this was. I questioned how I had given birth two times but this sickness was keeping me bedridden for so many days.

On the sixth day, my husband drove me to the doctor's office. I wore a mask due to my cough – I remember the nurse saying she could tell from my eyes how awful I felt. That's no shit. My temperature was taken – day six at 104 degrees. Concerns were expressed over such a high temperature for a long period of time. I was x-rayed; diagnosed with flu and pneumonia. Sent to the pharmacy for antibiotics, my drug of choice – the Z pack. It had turned me into Super Woman every time I had ever been sick. I waited days; it did nothing.

I continued to lay in bed – my body roasting, drenching the sheets with sweat, but I was so cold. Apparently, I smelled really bad. When people would come to check on me, it was not a good reaction. I could not smell anything. More days would pass. Mostly slept and coughed. A couple of texts and emails to my bosses and principals. I had to keep cancelling classes, I could not move and people were getting really concerned.

A full two weeks later, I had recovered enough to go back to work – at least so I thought. I went to classes for two days. Most of the faces were unrecognizable, I could not recall names of students and I had to sit down to lecture. I had no energy, coughed all the time and could barely function. It was Friday, March 13. We were heading into Spring Break. I promised them all I would be back to my normal self the next time I saw them. That's when the country shut down and we never went back to the classroom.

Back to the doctor the end of March for that awful cough – no advice other than cough syrup. And oh yeah, we reviewed those x-rays and you didn't have pneumonia. So, what do you think it is/was? Based on what's happening now, we would say you had COVID. Yeah, whatever – that's impossible.

Another month goes by. Something is off. I am no longer myself.

I cannot remember people's names. I am repeating myself all the time. I ask the same question over and over. I am driving my family crazy – it is like I have early onset Alzheimer's. When I try to talk, my brain glitches and the words won't come out. I am getting lost driving in places I have known my entire life. My attention span used to be focused like a programmed robot, now I cannot keep at one thing for very long. WTH.

It was the middle of May when I went back to my primary care physician. At this time, there was nothing in the media about the cognitive issues from having COVID. There was fear I had a stroke. Heck, Google your symptoms and literally every symptom known to man will lead you to a cancer diagnosis. Can't hear? Have cancer. Can't sleep? Have cancer. Limp when you walk? Have cancer. That's it - I must have a brain tumor. Or, I have used too much Advil PM and that's known to cause mini-strokes if taken over a long period of time. I was sent for an MRI.

I was terrified of going into that tube. No one told me the contrast dye makes you feel like you pee yourself. I am alone in a tube with a broken brain – and now I have pissed my pants.

When the scan came back, no one knew what to do with me. I was a medical mystery. There was inflammation and I was told my scan looked like the brain of a sixty-year-old. I was barely forty – that's great news. So, let's Band-Aid fix her. Let's hop her up on steroids for the inflammation and Ritalin for the attention issues. I declined their Ritalin but did do a round of steroids. Steroids and I are not friends – never have been, never will be. My eyes get as big as half dollars, I can't sleep, I eat everything in sight and I get mean. Like really, really mean. My physician didn't know what to do, so off to neurology I went. Lots of tests, like hours and hours of cognitive testing.

The results were terrifying.

I was given my newest label: "COVID long-hauler".

I was an award-winning professor and I had lost my mind. I was sinking into my own personal version of hell.

I could not think of five words that started with a certain letter. I could not remember details from stories being read to me. I couldn't do the problem-solving puzzle games. I could not draw what they asked me to. I can't even remember what most of the tests were. I do remember the woman proctoring the tests had a shiny necklace and I liked it. I was so easily distracted by everything during this time period – her jewelry was my focus. Makes perfect sense, right? Both my arms would occasionally go numb and my right hand had a tremor. It is stupid hard to try to put puzzles into some dumb pattern using only your right hand when it is trembling and you can't remember shit. I will forever hate those puzzles. One of the drawing ones showed up later in a Malcolm Gladwell book I was reading. Stupid puzzle. I went digging and finally found it for you:

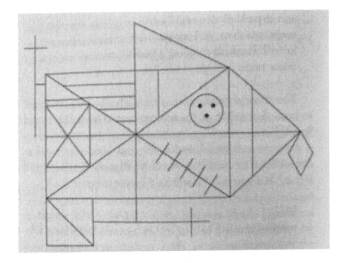

You get to stare and it and copy it first. The proctor removes it from your view and you draw it the best you can from memory. Evidently most adults do well at this – as do children but using different processes. Let me tell you, I failed miserably. (Just for kicks, give it a try, if you want.)

My distracted driving caused me to wreck my car. I was put on driving restrictions. I could not travel alone, in the dark or in heavy traffic areas.

My senses were off. I could not judge distance very well and was constantly hurting myself. My sense of pain was also off, so I would not realize I was hurt. I bashed my head with a crowbar while working outside. Had no clue, until my husband saw blood running down my forehead. I walked into cabinet doors, tripped over curbs. I was kicked in the dead center of my back by my horse, perfect hoof print (pretty cool, actually - was hoping for a scar - no dice) - didn't know I had been kicked. She flung me across the pasture, but I never fell down. Thank goodness, or I would have been trampled. Couldn't tell my food was hot and burnt the inside of my mouth - pretty badly - nasty infection that required antibiotics. (It was Long John Silver's chicken, delicious but not really worth it.) My vision had changed. I had to start wearing cheaters when I read. I had to get a laptop with a bigger screen. I stood on fire in the yard with my foot burning on the bottom and did not notice. I severely sliced open the end of my finger on a metal door knob and didn't have a clue.

One of the other strange effects during this time was not only failure to react to physical pain, but no physiological response to danger. Normally when you nearly collide into another car, your adrenaline kicks in. You start to shake. Something. We were nearly run off the road, my husband was visibly shaking. I felt nothing.

During the summer months of this time period, we were building - as in, doing it ourselves - a new barn for my horses. I spent day after day climbing a ladder and being ten feet in the air. It is no wonder that I am not dead. A bird would fly by, I would be too busy watching the bird to remember I was on the ladder. I hate heights anyway, but the things I will do for my animals is obviously absurd. I would go to find a tool and forget what I was looking for. I was supposed to be writing down lists and just doodled all over the scrap wood instead. I have a series of photos during this process that I have no recollection of taking. Apparently, I really liked to take photos of my feet. Black Converse.

I also spent many hours on the back end of a motorcycle without a sissy bar. As I type this, I can see how incredibly stupid I sound. I was in no condition to be on there and someone should have stopped me. I was clueless where I was most of the time. I would forget to hold on. I would wiggle nearly dumping the bike. Also, photos taken of me that I have no recollection of taking or where in God's creation I was at.

Memory is one of my favorite things to teach about in my psychology courses. We trust the things we remember to be true. However, our memory is not like a recorded version of events (not cassette tape, VHS tape, Beta tape or even your favorite mix tape). It changes. It changes based on the other things people tell us, other events we see – and the worst of the worst: false memories. False memories are the ones that our brain creates that are well – duh, false. Totally made up. They are very real and can lead you to believe they are indeed, fact. Just when I thought I could not sink any lower, I was rearranging chairs on a ship that was going down.

It was Sunday, August 2, 2020. I only know this from scrolling back in my camera roll. We had trimmed the Japanese Yews that surround our house. Being the great worker I am, I loaded my wheelbarrow and dumped it multiple times into the goat area for them to munch on.

There were six little goats living in this pen at the time – Ben, Colbert, Kit Kat, Betty, Thunder and Rain. A while later, Ben (my favorite of them all) was making a lot more baaa – baaa goat sounds then he normally did. He must be really happy. We left for a couple of hours that afternoon. When I returned home, Ben was incredibly bloated and dead. Yes, dead. He had always been the runt, had medical issues from the day we got him and a drama king. I thought it was odd and had to tell the kids he had passed away. I sobbed; I adored that damn goat. Evening turned to bedtime and I called it a rotten day. This probably sounds cold but if you have livestock, you know that things sometimes just happen. Sickness, weather, attacks by wild animals.

I got up the next morning and headed out to the barn for my morning chores. It was a Monday (based on my photo records) and I remember it was foggy. Bear with me as I share this portion of my life with you – it is going to be horrific – traumatic – and damn near unbelievable. I want to let you in on my thoughts as the events unfolded, as an outsider reading you cannot begin to imagine what is about to happen to my animals and myself.

As I walked out to the horse barn, I noticed two goats asleep in their little house. Their legs were sticking out of the doors. I had never seen them sleep like that - so stiff and exhausted. They always got up and talked to me, every morning. I kept heading to the horse barn. When I circled my way back two of them were still motionless. A couple others had started to cry. Colbert and Kit Kat were dead. Their bellies were extremely bloated and flies were attacking them. I panicked. Of course, I did. What was going on? What was different? Three dead goats in twelve hours. The bush clippings. Couldn't be that. I have done it for years. I removed the bodies from the area. A few minutes later, I would do a Google search on Japanese Yews and goats. Highly toxic, severe, fatal, deadly, one mouthful can kill a horse. Insert the tragedy of false memory right now. I had never, EVER fed my animals this plant before. I had vivid memories of doing it at my current home for over a decade and my prior home. THIS NEVER HAPPENED. This would be the moment that I stopped trusting everything my brain was telling me. I was unsafe to care for others and myself.

It gets worse. Way worse.

I removed the other three goats - Rain, Betty and Thunder from the pen and put them out with the bigger goats and horses. Rain was fine. Betty was bloated and having some twitching. Thunder was bad, like really, really bad. He was twitching and falling down, seizure like and unable to breath. I am alone in my pasture, out of my mind. I am crying hysterically. I cannot believe the neighbors couldn't hear me. My children are asleep. My husband left for work. I am alone. I frantically look online for things to do to help. Getting them to a vet is not an option, it is far and I cannot drive them alone. It is about 6:30 in the morning – again based on my photos that I don't recall taking.

Rain was never ill and she is still with me today. She must have not consumed any of the clippings.

Betty pulled through, barely. There were a couple of times I thought I was going to lose her but she is fighter. I call her Betty Badass now and always will.

Thunder will forever haunt me. I did everything I possibly could to save him. Working on his dying body in the pasture went on for about a half an hour, but it felt like a lifetime. I will spare you the dreadful details. I will never unsee what happened to him. What I did to him. It is on replay in my mind. He died in my arms.

No sooner than I was able to collect myself on the trauma I had just endured, I realized we had also dumped a couple tractor loads of bush clippings in to the horse pasture. Panic struck again. I did not know how to operate the tractor. I had been shown, but wasn't recalling the directions very well. Somehow, I managed to get it out there and get the rest of the clippings where no animals could reach them. All my animals were finally safe.

My girls would be waking up soon and I would have to tell them what happened. This was not like telling a child their overpriced goldfish from county fair is floating in its bowl. Kids – hell, adults – cannot wrap their head around what happened that morning. I have such a love for animals. I would never in a million years harm one. This day completely broke me. Whatever light I had left in me – any glimmer of hope – burnt out.

Finding Light in the Darkness

It was a week after the goat incident what I was finally seen in the neurology department. Since I had started documenting my medical journey, things were starting to come out in the media about the long-term impact of COVID and the cognitive problems. My test scores – and biggest failures – were indicative of what national studies were showing. There was nothing anyone could really do for me. I just need to continue to adapt. I set timers for everything, I made lots of lists. I practiced saying things out loud so I could recall it easier later. However, I was not able to find any mercy for myself. My mental health continued to plummet. My greatest fear was I would no longer be able to teach – or at least not as well – as I had in the past. I felt everything I had worked so hard for . . . slipping away . . . and there was nothing I could do to stop it.

The new academic year was upon us and the country was still partially shut down. I would be teaching the 2020-2021 school year from home. This was a blessing in disguise. I have no doubt that this change in modality allowed me to have the time I needed to recover without completely destroying my reputation.

I would continue to feel embarrassed and ashamed of what was happening to me. Even as some aspects of my health were improving, my state of mind was not. I hid from as many people as I could. I would eventually find refuge in joining a Facebook page (one of many examples of my love/hate relationship with social media) for COVID long haulers. In the media, the long-hauler numbers were growing rapidly. However, we were also under a lot of scrutiny. Some reports were comparing us to people with Munchausen Syndrome. On a clinical level, Munchausen is disturbing. On a personal level, the accusation is offensive. This is not a fake illness. Fake virus. Fake news. This is real life, impacting millions of people – and I have the medical documents to prove it.

Munchausen Syndrome is a mental condition where people create fictious symptoms in order to get attention. You may have heard of Munchausen Syndrome by Proxy – this is when someone makes another person intentionally ill – because they want to the attention of being the savior. This appears in the news every few years – usually mothers doing horrible things to their children – just to get sympathy and attention for having a sick child. Gypsy Rose Blanchard was a famous (extreme) case in the news a few years ago.

For months I scrolled through Facebook posts created by my 'friends' suggesting the virus is not real. It was all created for social control. People mocking those who have been incredibly ill. It is "just like the flu" or "a little cold." Complaining about not being able to go to their local bar, stuck wearing a mask, or missing a concert. Many of the early outbreaks had come from small events that never needed to happen. Women were giving birth alone. People were dying alone in hospitals. But people could not miss a prom party or bonfire. I became bitter and angry. The fear I mentioned earlier, coupled with resentment, was not a healthy place to exist.

I feel it important to say that everything that was happening to me medically and psychologically was not the result of seeing it on television and then deciding I had that, too. I was a few weeks ahead of what was being reported in the media. I would not have wished the pain I endured during this time of my life on my worst enemy.

A little over year into my journey, I joined Survivor Corps – a page for long haulers such as myself. People were able to share their stories and talk to others going through the same things.

This is what I said to 160,000 complete strangers on March 25, 2021:

I am a COVID Long Hauler. I have publicly hidden this for nearly a year. I bounce between being ashamed and angry, frustrated and defeated, and feeling as if I am literally crazy. I live in constant fear. I do not know what each day will bring for my body. As I write this - over 545,000 Americans have lost their lives to this virus. I am thankful to even be alive. As more stories are being shared, I realize that telling mine may help others. I hope sharing my story brings you some comfort. Perhaps you can help me find some inner peace...

I have long-term neurological, respiratory, and digestive problems. None of these existed prior to having COVID. I used to be a very healthy, energetic woman. I am a wife, mother, and college professor. My doctors do not understand what is happening and aren't seeking answers to try to help me. As an educator myself, this appalls me. My career is built on helping others learn, grow and flourish. I feel that doctors should do the same.

For months, the brain fog was overwhelming. It was like I had dementia – at age 40. I would repeat myself, ask the same things over and over, get lost while driving and forget things almost immediately. I would get distracted easily and could not concentrate on anything. I lost my depth perception and was always hitting my head. My cognitive tests last summer were an embarrassment. Things that used to come easily for me became really tough. I became hard to live with. I was annoying, even to myself.

On the worst day ever, my brain remembered feeding bush clippings to our goats. I had a very vivid memory of doing this for years, so without hesitation I dumped a wheelbarrow full. I also got lost while driving that day and forgot I was on the backend of a motorcycle. My brain was not working reliably and the clippings were poisonous. I, obviously, had never fed them before. I accidentally killed four of our goats. Can you imagine what it feels like to realize what you have done and explain it to your crying child? That was the day I stopped trusting myself. I lived in that space for a long time. I suffered - nearly in silence. I was (and still partially am) embarrassed. I know none of this is my fault – and I didn't do anything wrong to get this way – but that does not make it feel any better...

I best explain this period of my life as losing my joy...watching it slip away more and more each day. I was (before I got sick – gosh, I say that all the time and I hate it) an almost annoying, overly happy person. I have had to fight really hard to not completely lose myself during the past few months. The neurological issues have improved, but there are days where things just still aren't working right. People who did not know me prior my sickness may not even notice. But I notice. And I hate it.

The lingering issues seem to fluctuate between my brain, my lungs and my gut. Somedays it is all of it. It feels like my body is under attack. I never know what the day will bring. My recent CT scan shows permanent damage to my lungs. I never lost "the cough". I get winded just walking to the mailbox. Somedays lecturing takes my breath away. Somedays I cannot eat. It's like I just can't handle digesting anything – and there is no consistency in the food that sets it off. I have an arm that goes numb. The hand tremor has, thankfully, ceased.

I find myself battling to be even half the woman I was before I got sick. Daily. It is exhausting. I miss her. I am sure my family does, too. I am trying really hard to embrace the 'new' version of me. Somedays are just incredibly challenging. Seeing the "it's not real", "they are making it up" or "it's just like having a cold" mentality from people in our society does not help either.

Thank you for reading my story. I appreciate you. Advocate for yourselves and please take care...

The outpouring of love from strangers was remarkable. One reader expressed she had recently done something that scared her child – she did not go into detail. She thanked me for sharing my story and used it to help her family find comfort in her own recent unexpected behavior.

Within a couple days of my post, I was contacted by Sheila Hamilton, a mental health reporter out of Seattle, Washington. She asked me to do a Podcast for her show, *Beyond Well.* I was very hesitant; it is terrifying to share my truth with whomever would listen.

However, I decided it was time to change the narrative. I didn't want COVID to own me anymore. I wanted my life back. As an educator, I wanted to take my story and use it to help others. If you want to hear it in its entirety, you can Google it. I am episode 135.

Beyond Well

with Sheila Hamilton

(Image used with permission of Sheila Hamilton)

Life Goes On . . . For Some

I would have nearly two years of ongoing health problems. My cognitive issues finally seem to be a thing of the past and my cough has slowly lessened over time. Most days I feel like I am back to my old self. However, it is really strange that there are months of my life that I cannot recall. Some horrible things happened during this time period and those events torment me. I keep repeating to myself that old motto about 'what does not kill us makes us stronger'. Easy to read on a coffee mug - but hard to live by sometimes.

I would teach from home for a total of 521 days. Classes via Zoom, the internet dropping out, dogs barking at the Amazon van, family members wandering around. It was not what higher education should look like, but I did my best. We all did the best we could during these unprecedented times.

I got a cat for the first time since I was a little kid. We were shut-in's together and I became slightly obsessed with him. Duh, look how cool he is...

I spent nearly a year and a half of my life barely leaving the house. When it was time to go back for the 2021-2022 academic year, in person, I was terrified. Not first day jitters, but sheer terror. We lived most of that year in masks.

When the mandate was lifted, I had not seen a student's actual face in nearly seven hundred days. The pandemic has impacted all of us in some way. It changed the course of higher education for students and educators. It has forever changed me. I am thankful to be alive. At the time of this writing, the death toll in the United States has surpassed one million people.

Briefly Reflecting on The Long Haul:

The first thing that comes to mind when thinking about this portion is the song from *Smokey and the Bandit*, "East Bound and Down":

'We've got a long way to go and a short time to get there.'

Isn't this lyric representative of humanity as a whole?

This section was only about three years – which is such a tiny fraction of my lifetime – but the impact will last forever. I am a firm believer that we are not given more than we can handle.

'We gonna do what they say can't be done.'

All of my experiences thus far would prepare me for my cruise down . . .

Part Five:
The Road Less Traveled

While I Was Cleaning the Closet

On Christmas Day 2020, two of my friends lost their husbands. One died from a medical emergency and the other took his own life. One of the themes throughout this book is the essence of time and the lives people are living parallel to each other.

It was a cold day in January and I was knee deep in my walk-in closet. Sorting through the shoes I have not worn in a decade and the pile of meaningless t-shirts that I refuse to part with.

At that exact same time, one of my friends was burying her husband. Please do not think poorly of me that I was not in attendance. This was in the heart of the pandemic and funerals were very limited. Otherwise, I would have been there.

A few hundred miles away, two little boys were having their first day back to school after their father committed suicide. I cannot imagine what it is like to be the wife or child in this situation. I mean, honestly, unless you have ever been there – how could you?

Another theme throughout this book is the importance of destigmatizing – and start talking. In the past few years, I have known nearly a dozen people who have taken their own lives. Suicide rates throughout the United States have been steadily on the rise the past couple of years - especially in young adults. It is important to address this as an epidemic in our country.

Conversations about mental health are so important and are becoming more prevalent. However, many of the people who really need support and help are not the ones talking. They are smiling, hiding in plain sight and slowly drifting away.

As we age, we start to view death differently. I would say in my earliest adulthood years - when I was behaving stupidly most of the time - I was fearless. I did not have any real concern for my own life or regard for the lives of others.

After having my daughters, things shifted - it was all about being around to take care of them. As I have entered middle adulthood, my concerns went from literally being around to wipe their nose to having an estate to leave behind. I want to be able to provide for them even after I have passed away.

I would assume this happens to most people as they age - even more so in elderly years. We think more about what will happen to our loved ones, how much time we have left, and we look back on our lives with either integrity or despair.

Getting incredibly ill and the lingering effects of COVID forced me to face my own mortality. About a year into my sickness, I was in the emergency room for severe abdominal pain and was pumped full of Fentanyl. This is a pain medication 50 to 100 times more potent than morphine. Many people are dying from overdoses due their street drugs being laced with it. I felt my airways close up. I could not speak or breathe. My eyes started rolling back in my head. My husband pushed the call button and no one came. He took off running and screaming searching for someone to help. It was terrifying.

Moments like this make you realize how precious life truly is. It can be taken away from you in the blink of an eye. Do not take anything for granted.

Midlife Quirks

It would be presumptuous of me to think all my readers are the same generation. Perhaps my lyrical references are lost on some of you. I apologize. However, I can tell one thing we all have in common: weird things make us happy as we age.

Mine are things like being able to shower without interruption. Making stupid references to movies and being dumbfounded when people do not immediately understand them.

Scented trash bags.

Finishing an entire tube of Chapstick without it breaking or getting lost.

Being seated near the restroom in restaurants.

When Huey Lewis comes on the radio – that's the best of all.

Amuse me...

We have been pretty serious with our boxes – list the strangest things you have learned to appreciate as you have gotten older:

The Apple Does Not Fall Far from the Tree

I have spent a lot of time fixated on the thought that my poor life choices would impact my daughters. Well, let's be honest: they have, they do, and they will. I have mentioned before that I have spent lots of time showing them exactly what not to do. My hope for the future is that my pattern of doing this is broken. I guess time will tell.

My oldest daughter got into a pretty serious relationship at a young age. At the time, I thought it was alright. He was a nice boy and they spent a lot of time at my home. I felt like she was safe and I knew what was going on. About a year in, things started to take a turn - which I was unaware of. It had turned controlling and toxic - honestly, on both sides. She was being emotionally and verbally abused on a daily basis. This would eventually turn physical.

The nice boy she had fell in love with had turned into a not so nice young man. He was lying often, using drugs and abusing alcohol. Her sixth sense knew something was wrong, which did indeed probably make her act somewhat neurotic while seeking honesty and answers. I was unaware he had started grabbing her and pushing her. The final straw would be the night she called me when he shoved her into a wall at his house. She was terrified.

Let me say, this is not my story – it is her story – being shared with her permission. I am including it due to the fact that I am so incredibly proud that despite my shit role modeling at times, she stands strong. Yes, she got herself too deep into something. But she stood up for herself. Even when we doubt our ability as a parent, we need to have faith in our kids.

Watching your child go through their first broken heart is worse than it happening to you. None of the words are the right words; you can't fix it. This was a rough one. The toxicity had soaked into her core. I slept in her bed for nearly week, she lost weight and cried more tears than the Mississippi River could hold. I didn't know if she was going to bounce back. But she did.

So many people have the misconception that teenagers do not need their parents. This is the furthest thing from the truth. Yes, they can feed and dress themselves (barely) but they still need our support mentally. They are incredibly hard to get along with a lot of the time and have tumultuous mood swings. It does suck. But they are out there handling really big stuff. In a world much scarier than what I grew up in. With non-stop communication and devices that are literally rewiring their brains. I am not saying be a helicopter parent – I am just saying don't stop parenting.

Part of the abuse my daughter endured happened right under my roof. When I was home. This is alarming. They hide things – and they are good at it.

The number of teenagers and young adults that are suffering from depression and anxiety is at an all-time high. Check on them – the bridge between childhood and adulthood is the hardest one to cross. Help them build the bridge before they accidentally burn it down.

Teenage Drama Queens

I have two of them. I deserve every bit of shit they give me and I try to take it the best I can. Overall, they are good girls and have not made the horrible decisions that I did at their age(s). I am incredibly proud of them – even on the days they are nearly impossible to be around.

It is really hard to parent teenagers - you can preach until you turn blue in the face but they are still going still to do whatever they decide. We have had our fair share of trouble. My oldest would get caught sneaking in past curfew. (I was savage and laying in her bed in the dark when she crept in. I highly recommend doing this. Amazing.) She also has a lead foot like her mother and had two tickets in too close of a time period. (Check your state laws, they don't play with new drivers and will legit take your kids' license away.) She was the only one in her high school to have this happen. Hence, she was a learning lesson for all and awarded "Best Driver" for her senior award. I am so proud.

On the flip side, she earned her CNA license while in high school and is heading to nursing school this fall. She has a big heart and loves to help others.

My younger daughter hit a deer the day after she got her driver's license, then was in an accident a month later with her sister. She has refused to drive ever since. I mean, I can't blame her – but I never thought I would be hauling both of them around at this point (even momentarily) in their lives.

But – we do – we do whatever our kids need – at the inconvenience of ourselves and everyone else.

I will never be able to understand the bond between these two. They are polar opposites and barely speak to each other most of the time. In the blink of an eye, they are picking on me together and spending the day shopping. I don't get it. But really, I am not supposed to. I don't have that sister bond. I am glad they have each other. I hope when they are grown and move out that they are friends, but who knows. I don't get to control that.

I think that is the hardest thing about raising kids – teenagers – is the loss of control. When they are toddlers, we can baby proof everything and make sure they are safe. We keep doing things as they age, but eventually we have to trust that we have done the best that we could. The world has shifted in the past four decades. I never thought I would be the mom that says things along the lines of "back in my day", but I do. I fear what it will be like for my children and grandchildren.

I would like to think I have prepared them (and will continue to do so) be to be kind, courageous and respectful young women. The three of us have done a lot of growing up together. Despite their mother being a "dropout" and a "drunk driver" – who forced them to grow up in a "broken home" - they are remarkable humans.

Greatest of All Time (GOAT)

I must share my favorite photo of Little Ben. He was kind of iconic. He went to junior high with one of my daughters for a demonstration speech. He crapped all over the school. It was great. I mean, shit does happen. Right? Here is Ben after our trip to the junior high. How can you not love that face – he actually posed for selfie...

Before I got sick, I felt like I inspired my students. I was open with them about everything. I used Ben's field trip as a way to reach out to them. I shared these thoughts:

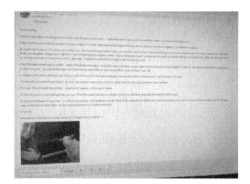

Hi Everyone,

I have a reputation of being the instructor who sends out goat pics.... I definitely don't want to let anyone down - so here is Little Ben and I.

After reading your Erikson answers on your exams, it is clear regardless what stage of life you are in....many of you are struggling...for different reasons.

So I wanted to share Little Ben's story with you. Ben was the goat I didn't want. He was the runt, his horn removal didn't go well and he needed more TLC than I wanted to deal with. Well, my daughter begged me and I gave in. Flash forward just a couple of months - Ben is still pretty small - a dog busts through our electric fence and attacks him. Literally uses his head as a chew toy when no one was home. It was bad. Thankfully, Little Ben is a fighter and recovered well.

Flash forward a few more months - when this photo was taken - Little Ben went to Fisher Junior High School to be part of my daughter's speech. She wanted to teach the class how to worm a goat. He was excited (and terrified) and pooped all over the school office. I had to clean it up. Yay.

I snapped this photo when we got home. Look at him. He is seriously smiling for the camera. Weird. Anyway, here are my lessons for you:

1) Life will try to knock you down - do your darndest to get back up. Every single time. Do not underestimate your abilities.

2) Crap - literally and figuratively - is going to happen - at the worst times.

3) Find the good in everything you can. This little goat has been a real pain in my rear. But he is seriously the sweetest little dude.

4) Face the things that you fear - or that challenge you. My daughter was terrified of ALL animals for YEARS and now she has goats and rides horses. If it had not been for her being a nag, we would not have Ben - or this motivational story to share with you.

(Posted on February 4, 2020)

If you check my Rate My Professor, it will confirm I have a reputation for sharing goat selfies. Truth. (Totally weird, but pretty proud of this.) I am also the mom who accidentally killed four her kids' goats. Truth. We must take ownership of all our truths, no matter how hard that might be.

And this would not be complete without a photo of Badass Betty. I have no recollection of taking this photo, but you can still see the pink Pepto Bismol on her mouth and nose that helped save her life on that dreadful day.

Baggage Claim

Well, folks. There you have it. While I have not
shared every aspect of my life with you – I have shared a lot.
I am hoping that you were able to relate to some of these
experiences. Perhaps you will learn from my mistakes and
avoid putting yourself into the situations I did. I do hope that
I made you laugh. In my lifespan development courses, I ask
my students the first week what is one aspect of aging that
they dread. Wrinkles is always a popular answer. I (as have
you) have earned every wrinkle – and laugh line – on our
faces. Laughter is one of the best medicines. Use it
excessively.

Writing this was incredibly challenging. It forced me
to circle back to many aspects of my life that I had left
behind a long time ago. However, it was also incredibly
therapeutic. I was able to find some common themes in my
life, pinpoint where certain behaviors began, and find some
insight that will be helpful for my future.

You cannot close the door on chapters of your life if
you do not process them fully. They will come back to haunt
you, trust me.

For many years I carried the baggage and burdens of
others. You cannot mentally handle and process the things

that are happening to you if you are constantly carrying everyone else's load. I know, first hand, how hard it can be to let somethings go. I encourage you to stop carrying the luggage of all the people you love and to start unpacking your own suitcase. One day at a time - hour by hour, if that's what it takes.

As for me, well . . . I have no idea what the future brings. I expect to keep teaching for a few more decades. I would be lost without my students and the joy they bring to my life. My girls will grow up and start lives of their own. All the little things that annoy me now will become the things I will miss someday. I will probably try to mend my broken heart with another dog when that happens. Maybe two. My husband and I will grow old (him faster than me, he robbed the cradle) and keep working out the crap that drives each other nuts. Time will move along even faster than it has in the past. More lessons learned, more memories made, more laugh lines earned and more tears shed.

I started writing this memoir multiple times over the course of four years. Life just kept happening. Hard stuff. Great stuff. Life changing stuff. I do believe we go through everything for a reason, even if we don't know what it is at the time. I also believe humans are amazingly resilient creatures. It has been incredibly interesting while writing, to go back and pin point exactly where some things shifted – for better or for worse. Of course, we cannot necessarily see the impact in the moment, but there is beauty in finding it later. There is forgiveness. There is closure.

If I have in any way inspired you, helped you, opened your eyes to things, made you laugh, yell, or cry – please reach out to me (camcara21@yahoo.com). One of my favorite things is learning about the lives of others. I would love to know more about you.

I appreciate you for taking time to reminisce with me – to grow with me – and for reading. I hope that sharing my path while seeking mercy has helped shine some light on yours...

To be continued . . .

Epilogue

Because I have the best parents on the planet and their sense of humor amazing (they are also slightly losing their shit due to age, but we are going with it) – my dad agreed to pose in THE Illini jacket for you. He checked - there is no weed stashed in the pocket. Thanks, Carl. We appreciate you.

About the Author

Cristina received her Bachelor of Arts and Master of Science degrees from Eastern Illinois University and completed her post graduate studies at Illinois State University. She is an interdisciplinary scholar teaching college courses in psychology, sociology and family science. She was awarded Illinois Council on Family Relations Family Mentor Award in 2018, Heartland Community College's Outstanding Adjunct Faculty Member Award in 2019, and Illinois State University's Impact Award in 2020. She is a Certified Family Life Educator (CFLE) through the National Council on Family Relations.

Her research interests formerly include the impact of divorce on children and juvenile delinquency. Her more recent area of focus has shifted to incarceration in the United States. This includes examination of systemic injustices, the history of American penitentiaries, wrongful conviction, rehabilitation and recidivism.

She resides in Central Illinois with her family.

You can reach out to her at: camcara21@yahoo.com

Made in the USA
Middletown, DE
09 July 2022

68862026R00126